The
East Sussex
Village Book

THE VILLAGE BOOK SERIES

The
East Sussex
Village Book

RUPERT TAYLOR

with illustrations by Jo-Anne Taylor

COUNTRYSIDE BOOKS

NEWBURY

First Published 1986
© Rupert Taylor 1986
Reprinted 1988
All rights reserved. No reproduction
permitted without the prior
permission of the publishers:

Countryside Books
3, Catherine Road,
Newbury, Berkshire.

ISBN 0 905392 59 0

Cover photograph of Firle
by Mark Roe

Produced through MRM Associates
Reading

Printed in England by
J.W. Arrowsmith Ltd., Bristol

County of EAST SUSSEX

FOREST ROW

ASHDOWN FOREST

WADHURST

N

HEATHFIELD

R. OUSE

R. ROTHER

RYE

BATTLE

R. CUCKMERE

RYE HARBOUR

LEWES

HAILSHAM

HASTINGS

BRIGHTON NEWHAVEN

EASTBOURNE

Introduction

This is not primarily a guide book. It will not tell you the most scenic route from Battle to Brightling, or which days Michelham Priory is open to the public or where to find the flakiest sausage rolls between Hammersmith and Hastings.

It concentrates on the feel rather than the appearance of a village. In place of geography and gastronomy, uplift and architecture there is a little history, a pinch of legend, the odd anecdote and a swarm of characters, good, bad and indifferent, who have left their mark on our rural life. It is a book as much about the past as what goes on today.

The eccentrics, you will find, play a prominent role. This is not simply a quirk of my own; in compiling the book I have discovered that it is the larger-than-life figures, however humble their background or achievements, that become a proud feature of local folklore faster than those more worthy sons and daughters of Sussex who have earned fame through art, writing and inventions.

I began to really get to know the county of my birth as the youngest reporter on the staff of the local newspaper when in an office of non-drivers my moped was pressed into relentless service, taking me to parish councils, fetes and flower shows. It built an abiding affection for those particular villages and their people, and prompted me (when I had four wheels) to discover those further afield.

The books on Sussex are legion, and many would argue that the ensuing pages can only scratch the surface of each place. But I hope that in doing so some of their atmosphere will be conveyed and, perhaps, you will discover something you did not know before.

I am indebted to numerous individuals across the county who have been helpful and patient in my quest for information, and particularly to the ladies of the East Sussex Federation of Women's Institutes, whose knowledge of 'their patch' has been invaluable.

Undoubtedly I have left out a lot which deserved recording and even got the yarns all wrong in some cases. For this I apologise, and eagerly await any additions or corrections that readers care to send me.

Rupert Taylor,
Framfield, 1986

ALCISTON

Alciston

Plenty of energy is required if you come here on a Good Friday because you may be required to join in the village's tradition of skipping outside The Rose Cottage pub. Not the conventional sort of solo skipping either ... here the participants form a line while a long rope is swung over their heads and hopefully under their legs by two people at either end.

This particular rite of spring is believed to have its origins in the rope with which Judas Iscariot hanged himself after the betrayal of Christ. In a good year Alciston will have as many as 20 people jumping in unison in the lane beside the pub. As its name implies, The Rose Cottage was a private house until it started to quench the thirsts of the locals in the 1890s.

A'ston was the pronunciation for this downland village in the old days when it had a form of weather lore as reliable as any present forecast by satellite and computer, even if it gave slightly shorter notice of when to go out with your brolly:

> 'When Firle Hill and Long Man wear a cap,
> We at A'ston gets a drap.'

The single street of old thatch and timber houses ends at the foot of the Downs in a duck pond, the church and a farm which incorporates the remains of a 14th Century abbey. This dependency of Battle Abbey was once a sort of holiday camp for the monks who came here for rest and retreat. The remains of their dovecote have been restored by villagers.

The medieval tithe barn is enormous and still, happily, serving the purpose for which it was built. It is about 170ft long and is claimed to be the largest tithe barn in the county. Somebody once counted the number of tiles in the roof – there are more than 50,000 of them.

Alfriston

The price of being picturesque can be a high one. Alfriston, at the head of 'millionaire's valley' where the Downs give way on either side to the meandering course of the Cuckmere, has the sort of olde worlde charms that make it a magnet for visitors, but their presence means a massive traffic snarl-up in the narrow main street during the summer months.

Coaches full of day-trippers are blamed as the main culprits for the congestion and causes something of a rift in the community. Some residents are all for the quiet life but the folk with antique, gift and tea shops to run depend on tourists for their livelihood. A proposed ban on coaches entering the village from the south caused uproar among traders in 1985, who maintained it would affect the economy of the village.

Tourism has brought a boom in Alfriston's latter day fortunes and is in many ways a renaissance of the heyday during the Napoleonic Wars when the threatened invasion by the French brought a large number of troops to the area. The village catered for them with such traders as a brewer, cooper, glover, harness maker, malster, ropemaker, shoemaker, soap-boiler, tallow chandler, tanner and even a peruke maker, who all prospered. The bubble burst with Wellington's decisive victory at Waterloo in 1815.

There was another trade for which the village was notorious. Most of the population seem to have been involved in smuggling, but the best-known exponents were the desperadoes who followed one Stanton Collins, leader of the Alfriston Gang.

Collins was the son of respectable parents and lived at The Market Cross Inn, now (what else) The Smugglers. This unique building, with its 21 rooms, 48 doors, six staircases and various hiding places and hidden exits, was the ideal headquarters for the illicit business to be carried on without fear of discovery. With the Cuckmere flowing beside the village and the coast only a mile or two away at the river's mouth, they were in an ideal spot to bring booty ashore and hide it away ready for transport and distribution inland. The gang was never caught but it was broken up when Collins was, ironically, arrested for sheep stealing in the 1830s and sentenced to seven years transportation. The last of the gang was Bob Hall, who died in Eastbourne Workhouse in 1895 at the age of 94.

Where other smugglers acquired something of a Robin Hood like persona, the Afriston Gang were a far more sinister bunch with a reputation for stopping at nothing. An old tale states that on one occasion the smugglers were in hiding on the cliffs overlooking Cuckmere Haven waiting for a signal from the boats that the cargo had been landed. Just as they were about to make their way down to the shore a Revenue Officer appeared on the clifftop, picking his way through the darkness by the large lumps of chalk set at intervals along the path. The smugglers had prepared for such a possibility and had moved some of the rocks so that they led directly to the cliff edge. The officer tumbled over with a cry but somehow managed to throw out an arm and cling to the edge. He looked up at the gang as they rushed from their hiding place and begged to be hauled up to safety, but one of the smugglers callously stamped on his fingers and sent him plunging to his death. Only a deathbed confession revealed the truth of what happened on that dark night; it had until then been held to have been an accident.

A more lighthearted incident occurred when a smuggler was hiding in a cottage near Market Cross with the Revenue men hot on his heels. There lived a woman who was expecting a baby. Friends hauled a pig from its sty and hid it with the man under the woman's bed. The officers searched the cottage and were about to enter the bedroom when the smuggler gave the pig a squeeze – it let out a squeal like a new-born babe and the officers discreetly departed.

Alfriston's battered market cross at the end of the main street makes it unique in East Sussex and the only other in the county is the far better preserved example of Chichester. It was probably erected here early in the 15th century for in 1405 Henry IV granted to 'the King's town of Alfryston' the right to hold a market on Tuesday in each week and two fairs annually on April 30th and November 29th. The original cross was hit by a lorry in 1955 and was so badly damaged that only a small portion of the stone could be used in its replacement.

The Star Inn, with its fascinating carvings and colourful ship's figurehead incorporated in the front of the building, has its origins in the 13th century as a resting place for pilgrims on their way to and from Chichester, and so lays claim to being one of the oldest inns in the country. The Old Clergy House, beside the village green known as the Tye, dates from the 14th century and was the first property bought by the National Trust in 1896 for the slightly ridiculous sum of £10. Restoration work cost more than £300. It has a separate room with no direct access to the house which was provided for the housekeeper of the priests, who before the Reformation were celibate.

In the days before the Conquest the bones of St Lewinna, a virgin Christian martyr killed by the Saxons, were kept at the church or monasterium at 'Alfriceston', and were held to have brought about many miracles. Their fame attracted a Belgian monk, one Balgerus, who stole the holy relics and brought them back to his own monastery at Bergue. There they remained until they were lost in the religious upheavals of the 16th century, though a rib bone of the noble Sussex maid was said to have survived in Flanders.

Maybe it was the memory of St Lewinna that gave rise to the village custom of placing a wreath of white flowers upon the coffin of a virgin and afterwards hanging them in the church. Even at the end of the last century as many as 70 'virgin garlands' were hung at one time in St Andrew's, famed as the Cathedral of the Downs.

While on the subject of the mortality of man (and woman) Alfriston is the last recorded place where a shepherd was buried with a piece of wool in his hand. It was done as a sign to St Peter that it was the shepherd's trade, not his lack of piety, that had made him an irregular church-goer.

The length of road leading from Dean's Place to Frog Firle is known locally as White Way and has a ghost story connected with the Chowne family. The words of an old song suggest the spirit is one of the Chownes:

> 'When evening closes in with shadows grey,
> And ghostly vapours overhang White Way,
> And Th' Crescent moon hangs gloomy in the west,
> 'Tis then the spirit of young Chowne can't rest,
> But walks abroad with melancholy stride,
> Adown the path that skirts the chalk hill-side'

Another version asserts it is the ghost of the young man's dog that was seen. In the latter part of the 18th century the heir to the

Chowne estate at Place House went for a walk one summer night with his pet and was set upon by thieves. Young Chowne resisted and was killed by a blow from a cudgel. After robbing the body the murderers hastily buried it, and also despatched the dog and buried it in the bank beside the road.

Seven years after the heir's disappearance a couple were out walking the same road when they saw a small white dog which to their amazement vanished into the bank. The phantom hound appeared every seven years after that until in the early 19th century the skeleton of a young man was discovered during road widening work near the spot where the dog had been seen to vanish. The fact that an old tramp had confessed on his deathbed to being one of the thieves left little doubt that the bones were the remains of the lost heir and they were taken to the churchyard and reburied. No phantoms have been seen along White Way since then.

Many years ago Alfriston had its own racecourse on the Downs, and long after it had ceased to be a haunt of the punters the village had a reputation for racehorse training. When James Harry Batho's *Longset* won the Lincoln in 1912 the whole village joined in the celebrations and the triumphant trainer presented every family in Alfriston with a joint of beef.

There was not such excitement again until October 27, 1943, when an enemy sea mine was discovered in the Cuckmere near the church. Most of the population was evacuated while the Royal Navy rendered the mine harmless.

Arlington

They answered to some strange names here nearly 400 years ago. Baptismal registers began in 1607 and contain more than a ring of Pilgrim's Progress about them, though the local offspring ceased to be lumbered with the oddities before Bunyan was born. Some of the more choice examples are: Morefruit Stone, Sin-Deny Earle, Zealous Foote, Patience Tester (!), No-merit Vinall, Thankful Foote and God's Blessing Bell.

In 1615 it was recorded: 'Baptized Stephen the son of John Williams, executed fortnight before for stealing.' (the writer adds

'God give his sonne more grace'). Later there is a sad little post-script: 'Buried Stephen the son of John Williams (the Lord will be more merciful).'

Arlington is fortunate in being the rare possessor of church-warden's accounts which date back to the 15th century. The chief interest lay in the herd of 30 cows owned by the church which were hired out to local farmers at a rent of 2lb of beeswax per cow per annum to supply light for the shrines.

The church of St Pancras is one of the most interesting in the county, with specimens of all periods of architecture from Saxon times onwards – including some Roman bricks, a legacy of the Roman road that passed through the village. Inside there is a 13th century food storage jar found under the floor a century ago and repaired, and a 12th century wooden chest whose boards are rough cut from the tree. It is hard to believe that this noble build-ing was for a long time in such a state of neglect that less than a century ago the Bishop was moved to describe it as being 'in a state of decay, dirt and ruin ... worse than any other church in Sussex ... devoid of every decent requisite of worship. During the Rev Thomas Burston's incumbency from 1889-1918 St Pancras underwent a major restoration.

The only serviceman from the village killed in the First World War, Jesse Levett, was commemorated by a plaque in the village hall nearly 70 years after his death. When villagers collected for a war memorial in 1920 they decided to spend the money on some-thing tangible and an Army hut was bought at Seaford, disman-tled and carted to the village to serve as the hall.

Friends were inspired to remember Jesse on the death of one of his brothers and they paid for the plaque, unveiled with due cere-mony and displayed with his medals while Arlington's oldest inhabitant, Mrs Amy Wooller, gave personal reminiscences of Jesse to the assembly.

Arlington's scattered parish takes in several contrasting fea-tures: The broad expanse of the local reservoir with its wildfowl and anglers; the roar and bustle of the Eastbourne Eagles speed-way track on race days; and the leafy solitude of Abbott's Wood, which has stood at least as long as the reign of Henry I (1100-1135) when it was owned by Battle Abbey.

Ashburnham ✣

Rather gruesome relics of King Charles I were kept in the village church here until late in the 19th century: the shirt, silk drawers and garters he wore at his execution, the sheet that was thrown over his body, his watch and a lock of his hair.

They were held to have healing powers to those who touched them, a belief that persisted until 1859 when a sick child was wrapped in the King's sheet at Ashburnham as a remedy for the scrofula.

The relics were brought here by John Ashburnham, for many years friend and servant to Charles I, who called him Jacko. This staunch royalist and former MP for Hastings was Groom of the Bedchamber, and accompanied the King on his flight from Oxford during the Civil War. At the Restoration in 1660 he got his old job back, serving Charles II and Samuel Pepys recorded in his diary how Jacko berated a subordinate who allowed his royal master to run short of handkerchiefs one day.

Ashburnham is a scattered and secretive community, hiding in its steep and twisting lanes two important reminders of the county's industrial past. Near Ponts Green was a brickworks with the last wood-fired kiln in Sussex, still in use until 1968, and near Ashburnham Forge was the last iron furnace to be worked in the county, where firebacks were the speciality. Various dates are given for the year in which it was extinguished for the last time, 1828, 1820 and 1813. The latter is probably the most accurate, for William Hobday, last surviving labourer at the furnace who died in 1883, asserted that work ceased forever in that year.

The history of the village is interwoven with the ancient family that bears its name. In the middle of the 12th century Reginals de Oseburnham was granting lands to the Abbey of Robertsbridge and seems to have been a considerable landowner in Ashburnham. Since then members of the family, with one short break of a few years, remained in occupation of the estate until Lady Catherine Ashburnham, the last of the direct line, died in 1953.

The church stands beside the family mansion, given to the Ashburnham Christian Trust as a centre for the training of lay members of the Church of England. The list of vicars begins in

1399 though there was probably a church here at a much earlier date because in 1374 one William, Vicar of Ashburnham, was excommunicated by the Bishop of Chichester 'for an unfortunate series of moral and ecclesiastical offences'.

Barcombe

There used to be a variation on the old theme of Sussex folk being strong in the arm and weak in the head which unkind neighbouring villages applied here: 'When the people of Barcombe want to make a cart, they make a waggon and saw it in half'.

The simple rustics of the past have been replaced by what 1980s jargon would describe as 'an upwardly mobile' community, but one that cares enough about its heritage (though not so much the bumpkin image) to revive maypole dancing outside The Royal Oak every May Day and to introduce a new angle on beating the bounds with a village fun run for charity.

There is enterprise here as well, with a workshop making snooker tables established in perfect anticipation of the meteoric rise in the sport's popularity and acres of blackcurrants which help satisfy the demand of the manufacturers of a well-known fruit drink.

Barcombe is really three villages in one, the old community near the church which was largely deserted when the Black Death ravaged the land, the populous Barcombe Cross which replaced it and Barcombe Mills near the now defunct railway line and the river Ouse.

The flour mill here by the river was mentioned in Domesday, and the last working mill was built on the site in 1870. It stood empty for many years after ceasing to grind corn until 1934 when it became a button factory, owned by a German and run by Italians as one of the major sources of employment in the village. But the war clouds were looming and the factory was completely destroyed by a mysterious fire in the early hours of Friday, March 10th, 1939. Sadly, several of the Italians who worked here died when the ship carrying them back to their native country was torpedoed by a German U-Boat after the outbreak of the Second

World War. Their ghosts are supposed to haunt the site of the old mill.

Percy Blackford, who still lives in the village, was a button polisher at the factory at the time it was destroyed. The buttons were placed in a giant drum full of reject matchsticks supplied by Bryant and May which was then revolved by water power (sometimes a turbine was used) and the friction produced a gleaming finished product. Still in Barcombe, too, is Stan Brooks, the last surviving fireman from the village brigade that rushed to the scene of the inferno that morning.

The nearby Angler's Rest has pictures on the walls which show the old mill buildings in their heyday.

Just up river was another mill, known to the locals in the early years of this century as the 'oil mill' where they made linseed-cake for the feeding of cattle.

Barcombe Mills was a popular spot for picnics on high days and holidays in Edwardian times thanks to its proximity to the station. It conjures up an attractive picture of mamas with parasols sitting on the riverbank with their children playing around them while the menfolk, in their shirt sleeves, indulged in a little fishing. The Ouse is tidal as far as here and occasionally sea trout are taken.

The first place in Sussex where road tolls were levied was over the village's Ouse bridge and the last recorded charges in 1939 show that getting from A to B could be expensive: Carriage and horses 1s; four wheels and horse 6d; two wheels and horse 6d; wagon and horses 1s 6d; steam engines 2s; motor cars 1s; motorbike and sidecar 3d.

Barcombe Place was at one time a Dr Barnardo's home for girls. Many of them married local men and settled down here.

Stoolball is a game played by sturdy Sussex girls, and this interesting variation on cricket with its square, upright wickets and round bats is largely confined to the eastern part of the county. It owes a big resurgence in popularity to a Barcombe man, Major W.W. Grantham KC, who between the wars was active in promoting stoolball for the benefit of men who had lost a limb in the First World War.

Beckley 🌿

Not a good place to have been a simple foundry worker at the height of the iron industry ... you might have found yourself on a forerunner of the treadmill. They made guns here and depended on water power to keep the bellows of the furnace going, so in dry winters when water was in short supply men had to literally 'tread the wheel', stepping from bucket to bucket to maintain blast and production.

Not a good place, either, to have held anti-Puritan sympathies 300 years ago. The Rev Thomas Sharpe and his wife lived at Church House and were so seriously assaulted by Cromwellian soldiers that Mrs Sharpe later died of her injuries.

Legend says that one of the murderers of Thomas-a-Becket, Sir Reginald Fitz-Urse, galloped from Canterbury to Beckley to seek sanctuary in the church, his right hand still covered in the blood of the Archbishop. In his desperation the knight overlooked the fact that treason and sacrilege had put him beyond the pale. The drumming hooves of his ghostly horse are believed to haunt the village on dark nights.

Beckley, left in King Alfred's will to his kinsman Osferthe, has one of the longest village streets in the county which is a gem for the enthusiast of architecture.

As well as guns, glass was made here in the past, formed into practical things like vessels, jars and bowls, and surely not serving any cosmetic purpose – it must be pure coincidence that there is a Glass Eye Farm in the parish!

Berwick 🌿

Art is often controversial and in this village the work of the paintbrush has caused a stir more than once. During the Second World War the Bishop of Chichester commissioned local artists Duncan Grant, Vanessa Bell and her son Quinten Bell to paint contemporary murals on the walls of the 12th century parish church. Their vivid pictures include a soldier, sailor and airman, the Annunciation and the Nativity, and incorporate the portraits of local personalities. The angels above the chancel arch have stylish 1940s hair-do's.

The redecoration met with some opposition at the time, but today the striking work makes the little village church a gem – and, after all, it was only a revival of the medieval practice of wall painting once so widespread but now reduced to mere fragments or lost forever in other villages.

Painting of a different kind also caused a row in more recent times. The weather-beaten pub sign outside The Cricketers needed replacing, but the W.G. Grace type bearded character that now marks the pub met with less than universal approval: 'Too gaudy,' cried the locals, but it is growing on them as time goes by.

Lightning can strike twice in the same place as Berwick church bears testimony. The spire was struck and destroyed in 1774 and in 1982 considerable damage was caused to the repaired structure by ball lightning.

One of the more unusual organisations that once enriched the social life of the village was the Berwick Sparrow and Rat Club, which had the Rev J.T. Burns as both President and Chairman. It was designed to keep down the numbers of these creatures and also gave the menfolk the chance to earn a little extra cash with 6d per dozen paid for 'old sparrows' and 2s per dozen paid for 'old rats'. The younger brethren realised a little less.

There was also quarterly cash prizes of 5s, 3s and 2s being offered to the members catching the greatest number of sparrows and rats. But the rules of the club were strict: No member could qualify for a prize unless he had handed in a minimum of 60 sparrows and 15 rats; the prey had to be caught in the parish; and 'members found smoking in stackyards or on any premises whilst catching sparrows and rats, or loading shotguns with ordinary paper instead of stout wads shall be disqualified for all prizes.' Nobody is sure when this form of bounty hunting ceased to operate.

Bishopstone ✺

A distinguished Saxon church and pretty cottages grouped around a green, known locally as The Egg, which has escaped Seaford's suburban tentacles.

As the name Bishopstone implies, it was for centuries a sort of retreat for the Bishops of Chichester, who used to stay here until the 17th century. In 1324 one of them entertained Edward II for two days.

It was the bishops who built the first recorded windmill in Sussex, and possibly in England, in 1199. The mill has long gone, as has a mill of an equally ingenious kind built by the industrious Mr William Catt who harnessed the power of the sea to grind his corn at the Bishopstone tide mill.

This son of a farmer believed in hard work and thrift. He and his wife would begin their working day at 3 am and his principle was to earn a shilling and save a penny. In addition to establishing the tide mill by the sea a mile or so from the village he reclaimed much of the coastal wasteland to grow more crops.

The mill and the hamlet which sprang up around it are no more, having been used for comprehensive practice by the artillery during the Second World War, but the memory lives on in the name of Tidemills.

Mr Catt seems to have been a stern but benign patriarch and it was recorded that at one harvest supper an old retainer, probably made bold by drink, had the temerity to say 'Give us yer hand, sir, I love ye, I love ye, sir; but I'm damned if I bean't afraid of ye though!'

Bishopstone church's most striking feature is the Saxon porch with a sundial on its gable bearing the name Eadric. One of its parsons of the past used to do his bit for nature conservation in the days when farmhands supplemented their incomes by trapping wheatears. The tender-hearted clergyman would secretly visit the nets and release the trapped birds, but he also spared a thought for the frustrated catchers by leaving a penny for every wheatear he had released.

James Hurdis, born at Bishopstone in 1763, was both clergyman and poet. He became curate at Burpham, in West Sussex, where he wrote *The Village Curate,* and was later made vicar of his native village. His work was much admired and he went on to become Professor of Poetry at Oxford. At Bishopstone he wrote in praise of the place of his birth in *The Favourite Village* 'printed at the author's own press, Bishopstone, Sussex.'

Blackboys

The picturesque derivation of this unusual name is the condition of the charcoal burners when they emerged from the woodlands at the old settlement here. Less engaging but probably more accurate is that the name means Black Wood or Blake's Wood; and there is also a record of a Richard Blakeboy.

The Blackboys Inn, an old coaching establishment dating from the 14th century, has a variation on the old pub game of Ringing-the-Bull where the players try to land a ring hanging from a piece of cord to the hook on a huge bull's head mounted on the wall. Here a stag's head replaces the bull.

Ronald Shiner, the actor who starred in a string of West End farces including *Worm's Eye View* in the 1950s, retired from the stage to become landlord here.

It was another landlord who repeatedly fell into the trap set by Horace Beddington, *Sussex Express* district reporter for many years and a familiar character as he travelled from job to job in his pony and trap. Horace's ploy was stunningly simple and totally unoriginal, but it never failed to get him a free drink at The Blackboys which mine host grudgingly felt obliged to provide:

Landlord: 'Good evening, Mr Beddington, and what can I get for you?'

Horace: 'That's very kind of you to offer landlord. I'll have a pint of your best bitter.'

Bodiam

The fairytale castle must not blind us to another claim to fame. The Bodiam pancake races were held here every Shrove Tuesday for many years and at one time attracted the attention of the BBC.

They were started by the Rev Algernon Cottam. Most of the able-bodied adults took part and they ran tossing their pancakes along a stretch of Levetts Lane. There was a twist: Bodiam's runners were in competition not only with each other but with a village some 200 miles away in Lincolnshire where a friend of Mr Cottam had organised a similar frolic. Times were compared over the telephone at the end of the day and the village with the best figures won a silver cup. The pancake tradition, like 'Bodgem's' train service and the Guiness hopfields, has vanished in its old form though there have been attempts at the primary school to revive it.

Building on the castle was begun in 1385, when the technology of castle building was at its peak, to protect the upper reaches of the river Rother from possible incursions by the French who a few years earlier had mauled Rye and Winchelsea. But the arrow slits, cannon ports and 'murder holes' (through which missiles could be dropped through the ceiling on attackers) were never used in anger. The castle fell into decay, was rescued in 1829 by 'Mad Jack' Fuller (see Brightling) when a Hastings builder planned to demolish it, and was then restored by two later owners, George Cubitt and Lord Curzon, who presented it to the nation. Under the care of the National Trust it is now a breathtaking if incongruous part of this rolling landscape.

If this were the Continent or the USA, the castle would be surrounded by a plethora of hangers–on, in the form of shops and souvenir sellers. But this is Sussex (albeit that the Kent border is just an arrow shot away) and the nearest it came to 'commercialism' was an innocent advertisement in an Edwardian castle guide book which stated that tickets for admission to Bodiam Castle could only be obtained at The Castle Hotel, where 'large parties are constantly catered for ... inclusive charge to visitors from 9/- per day or from £2.12s per week. No extras for light or attendance. Meals served at separate tables.'

Bodle Street Green

When an old army hut costing £42 became the village hall in 1923 it added an extra dimension to social life. The village responded to new diversions enthusiastically, 150 packing the building to hear Mr Woolgar play a selection on his gramophone ... and Mr Young read a paper 'Is Music Beneficial to Cattle?' The WI was born and a newspaper cutting described a meeting when a 'most useful demonstration was given on how to make indoor slippers out of an old felt hat.'

But all was not serene at the rectory at about this time. The Rev Ferguson Reed resigned his living because he could not manage on a nett income of £4.6s a week. He told his parishioners in a letter: 'It is the wages of a plumber or a London policeman, or half what a collier gets ... I am compelled to live in a large house and keep up a position and live like a gentleman'. His protest seems to have had some effect because by 1927 the stipend had been increased to £321 per annum.

Edward 'Cocky' Wrenn was described in the 1871 census as postmaster and shoemaker. In order to collect the post he had to walk to Hailsham and back every day, relieving the tedium of his 14-mile journey by indulging his passion for reciting narrative verse. *Paradise Lost* and *John Gilpin was a Citizen* were favourites when he stopped off at the Five Bells beerhouse. This colourful character (who claimed kinship with Sir Christopher Wren) would also give his rendering of *England, with all Thy Faults, I Love Thee Still* to the Hailsham ropemakers for a penny.

The Isted family flit in and out of Bodle Street Green's picture down the centuries. They were certainly an enterprising lot. Edward Isted of Trumpets Farm took to iron digging as a sideline and found himself hauled before the Quarter Sessions at Lewes in 1638 because he had done so much damage to the road from Bodle Street to Woods Corner that it had become both dangerous and impassable. He and his tenant, William Price, were ordered to repay the parishioners of Warbleton for the cost of the repairs.

In later years Edward's son John Isted appeared in a curious case before the Exchequer Chamber at Westminster because he had conveniently managed to 'lose' a 20-acre holding called Dill on which the rent was 4s. He lost his case and was ordered to pay the Lord of the Manor of Bucksteep the two years missing rent.

The threatened invasion by Napoleon in the early years of the 19th century brought vast numbers of troops to the area, men who must be fed ... and here were John and James Isted building a post mill to capitalise on the boom time.

Chicken fattening was big business in this area (see Warbleton) and the Isted family would not fail to make the most of it. A steam mill was started at Trumpets Farm in 1909, grinding the oats for delivery to the rearers and fatters.

The White Horse had a rather seedy reputation at the turn of the century; drunkenness and fighting made it a place you could not go 'without running into trouble'. But it had a good quoits team, playing across the road in what was then the pub garden. During the Second World War the distinctive white horse painted on the roof was ordered to be removed, because it would have provided a landmark for enemy aircraft.

Bodle Street nearly acquired a railway station on two occasions. In 1868 it would have been a halt on the proposed line from Hellingly to Hastings, and in 1896 it was included in a scheme to link Pevensey with the Kent and East Sussex Railway. If both plans had gone ahead the village could have been a railway junction today!

Brede ✤

The tale of the cannibal ogre has persisted for 400 years. Sir Goddard Oxenbridge, a towering 16th century knight, was said to eat a child every night for his supper. He could not be harmed by conventional weapons but was vulnerable to anything made of wood.

The children of Sussex held a council for self-protection and hit upon a plan. They persuaded the giant to become stupefied with drink and then sawed him in half with a massive wooden saw, the children of East Sussex riding on one end and their West Sussex cousins on the other.

The scene of the infants' deliverance, between Brede Place and the church, became known as Groaning Bridge and was haunted by the ghost of Sir Goddard. No doubt the story served two purposes: As a warning to naughty children from exasperated Brede mothers that the giant would have them on his plate, and an intimidating legend with which smugglers could scare away the curious from the nocturnal goings-on at Brede Place which they used as a headquarters.

But tales of the ghost and reports of strange noises at Groaning Bridge were well enough authenticated for the Psychical Research Society to take some interest in it at the beginning of this century. Poor old Sir Goddard lies in a tomb bearing his armoured effigy in the church he helped to build for the village, remembered still for his dining habits rather than his generosity.

Brede Place, which dates from the 14th century and is still sometimes referred to locally as the Giant's House, has another supernatural story. Alterations 300 years ago cut off the altar area of the chapel, disturbing the spirit of a priest who once lived there and who still haunts the spot where the altar used to be.

The house was rented for a time by Stephen Crane, author of The Red Badge of Courage (remember Audie Murphy in the film version?), and the sculptress Clare Sheridan also lived here. She carved a madonna from the trunk of an oak tree which is among the treasures of the church.

The village, pleasantly situated on a southern slope tumbling down to the small river which bears its name, was famous for its iron works, making cannon and shot until the bottom fell out of the Sussex iron trade. Brede went over to the manufacture of gunpowder in the 18th century and William Sinden was 'blown into five parts from the sudden explosure (sic) of Brede Gunpowder Mills, March 7, 1808.' Was he perhaps smoking on the job?

The vicar once found the actress Ellen Terry having a picnic lunch in the churchyard: 'The most cheerful churchyard I ever knew,' she told him. But it has a relic of a tragic Victorian love story in the form of a small oak cross bearing the single word 'Damaris.'

Damaris Richardson lived with her uncle in a modest cottage in Rectory Lane. She was a beautiful orphan who worked at the rectory and in a small residential school operated by Rev Maher to supplement his income. She fell in love with Lewis Smith, the handsome young son and sole heir of a wealthy Brede land-owner, and they would meet in secret at the west wall of the churchyard – she on the graveyard side and Lewis on the other, in the grounds of the big house where he lived with his parents.

They soon agreed to become unofficially engaged. But affairs are hard to conceal in a small village community and somebody told Lewis' father of the clandestine meetings. He angrily forbade any ideas of marriage – beautiful, charming and respectable Damaris might be, but she stood far below the station of the Smith family. Lewis, threatened with being cut off without a shilling, gave way to his father.

Presumably there was one final meeting of farewell beside the wall before they parted forever. Damaris, they say, died of a broken heart at the age of 22 and was buried near the trysting place on September 4, 1856. Her grave was unmarked until the Rev Aylward, who years later succeeded Mr Maher as Rector of Brede and remembered the orphan from his days as a pupil at the village's school, commissioned the erection of the cross. Lewis Smith never married, living alone and withdrawn in the big house he inherited. Villagers said he was often to be seen walking gravely in the gardens, close to the wall. He died, aged 65, on February 23, 1896 and was interred in the Smith family tomb on the north side of the church.

Brightling 🦢

Squire John Fuller of Brightling was dubbed 'Mad', 'Honest' and 'the Hippopotamus'; a larger-than-life eccentric who left an indelible mark on the landscape he loved. His famous follies ring the little village: the Temple, the Tower, the Sugar Loaf, the Pyramid and Brightling Needle.

The Fuller family made their money from the Sussex iron industry, suitably commemorated in the family coat of arms *Carbone et Forcipibus* (By Charcoal and Tongs), and John inherited the family fortune and the Brightling mansion, Rose Hill, on his 20th birthday in 1777.

He was large, he was outspoken, his style of dress was old-fashioned and he wore his hair powdered and pigtailed long after it had ceased to be the fashion. As the MP for East Sussex he had a stormy political career and his boisterous attitude often got him into trouble. During a heated debate he once insulted the Speaker by calling him 'that insignificant little fellow in a wig.' Another account describes Fuller leaping to his feet during a dull debate and in his sonorous tones describing the virtues of living in Sussex. After defying the demands to sit down for several minutes he left the totally bewildered House to return to Brightling in his heavily armed and well-provisioned carriage.

His days as an MP were numbered after a sensational outburst when the House was debating the ill-fated Walcheren expedition against the French in 1809. Fuller suspected a plot was being hatched against his king and country and hurled abuse at all and sundry. He was ejected from the Chamber twice, the second time in the custody of the Sergeant at Arms assisted by messengers.

He was offered the peerage for his philanthropy but refused it saying 'I was born Jack Fuller and Jack Fuller I'll die', which earned him the nickname 'Honest', while his enormous girth (he topped the scales at 22 stones) made him 'the Hippopotamus' to his fellow MPs.

The county as a whole owes a great debt to this colourful character. He bought the dilapidated Bodiam Castle in 1829 when it was due to be demolished by a firm of Hastings builders, thus preserving the great building for future generations, and he built the Belle Tout Lighthouse on the cliffs at Beachy Head near Eastbourne. He was also a great patron of the arts and sciences, giving £10,000 during his lifetime to the Royal Institution of Great Britain, and one of the greatest of England's painters, J.M.W. Turner was a frequent visitor to Rose Hill, his host paying large sums for paintings and drawings by the artist.

But it is for the Brightling follies that he is best remembered as 'Mad Jack'. He entered gleefully into their construction on his retirement from politics. Buildings apparently with no purpose but each with a tale to tell.

The Temple in the grounds of Brightling Park is a round building with a domed roof and Doric pillars in the Grecian style designed by Sir Rober Smirke. Local stories suggest it was used for gambling sessions or that it provided suitable privacy for the portly Fuller to cavort with giggling ladies of the night. Maybe it was just a nice spot to take tea on a summer's afternoon.

The Tower stands in a copse below the village making it almost invisible when the trees are in leaf. It is 35ft high, 12ft in diameter with a Gothic entrance, four windows and a top surrounded by battlements. Fuller is said to have built it so he could watch the repair work in progress at distant Bodiam Castle.

The Sugar Loaf can be found at Woods Corner, near Dallington, taking its name from its likeness to the shape in which sugar was delivered to grocers. Legend says Fuller made a bet that he could see Dallington church spire from his window at Rose Hill. When he discovered he could not he had a curious structure erected in a single night to look like the church top and win his wager. Inside The Sugar Loaf, saved from demolition by public subscription in the early 1960s, is a small room and in the 1930s an old man would describe how he once lived in it and brought up a family there.

A landmark for miles is Brightling Needle, or The Obeslisk, standing 65ft high at the second highest point in Sussex, 646ft above sea level. It was probably put up to celebrate Wellington's victory at Waterloo in 1815, though there is another theory that it marks Nelson's triumph at Trafalgar a decade earlier. Over the years it fell into disrepair and in 1985 the Needle took on the look of a rocket launchpad surrounded by steelwork when renovation work was under way.

Perhaps the most remarkable of the follies in Mad Jack country is The Pyramid, 25ft high and dominating the parish churchyard. It is a sobering thought that Fuller was preparing for his death 24 years before the event in 1834 and would look out of the window at his future mausoleum long before it was needed. It became generally accepted that he was interred sitting at a table in full evening dress with a top hat, a meal and a bottle of claret before him. The floor of The Pyramid was believed to have been scattered with broken glass to keep away the Devil. Repairs to the structure shattered that bizarre legend: No sign of Mad Jack was found inside (he is buried in the conventional way beneath the tomb) but on the wall was a verse from Thomas Gray's famous *Elegy*.

> 'The boast of heraldry, the pomp of power,
> And all that beauty, all that wealth e'er gave
> Awaits alike th' inevitable hour;
> The paths of glory lead but to the grave.'

The Observatory was another of Fuller's buildings, but it can hardly be called a folly. Mad Jack took a genuine interest in astronomy and it was fitted with the most sophisticated equipment of the day and contained a camera-obscura.

Fuller gave numerous gifts to the church including a barrel organ, the largest in Britain in working order, and on its installation in 1820 he presented the male members of the choir with white smocks, buckskin breeches and yellow stockings, and the females with red cloaks.

He was a village squire in the old paternal mould, providing work for the local unemployed by commissioning the building of a wall stretching for four miles around his land. The story has gone full circle and repairs to the wall are providing employment 150 years later.

The Green Man was the pub opposite the church in the centre of the village and it seems the vicar asked that it should be moved to take away temptation; the people were drinking instead of attending church. The new pub was established half a mile away from a converted barn owned, of course, by Mad Jack. It became The Fuller's Arms.

The church is dedicated to St Thomas a Becket. His festival was often kept on July 7th and it became the custom in Brightling to honour their patron saint with a wake or feast. On the Monday after July 7th the landlady of the inn would make light cakes to be sold in the morning and puddings in the evening.

Burwash

Alby Waterhouse has for many years had a proud but sad duty to perform for the inhabitants of Burwash. He turns on a light at the top of the war memorial on the evening of the anniversary of the death of each of the village's soldiers, sailors and airmen. There are some 100 names and dates recorded there so Alby is kept busy.

The original lantern which shone from the memorial tower beside the church was introduced at a time when there was no street lighting and the electric light of today shines just as bright in honour of the men who never came home.

The memorial was opened after the First World War by the man whose name has become synonymous with Burwash, the writer Rudyard Kipling. Tragically, among the names it bears is that of his son John, who was killed at Loos in August 1918 six weeks after his 18th birthday.

Kipling moved to Batemans, an old ironmaster's house, in 1902 and lived in the village for 34 years. He moved from Rottingdean to escape the crowds of admirers and sightseers who congregated there and found here the peace he had been looking for. This was despite the attentions of one particularly enthusiastic group of fans who set up what they called The Kipling Room in a local inn.

The locals came to know Kipling as a retiring, kindly man and small boys were in later life able to recall that they were allowed to fish in the stretch of the Dudwell which runs through the grounds of Batemans, and that they were told stories by the writer which were later published. When he went abroad he never forgot to send the young anglers postcards.

Kipling loved gadgets of all kinds and soon after moving to Burwash he adapted the 18th century watermill in his grounds to power a generator which supplied electric light to the house until the 1920s. The mill was restored in recent years to perform the job it was originally intended for.

Batemans, built by John Brittan in 1634, has been described as 'the loveliest small house in Sussex'. It is certainly a very large small house and is now owned by the National Trust and kept much as the writer left it. The story goes that Mr Brittan promised his workmen 'Christmas fare as long as the oak log lasted', and the furnace-men saw the chance of a real beanfeast at their master's expense. They found the biggest, most gnarled oak on the estate, cut a huge log from it which they soaked in the river for a week then rolled it triumphantly to Batemans.

There it hissed and spluttered in the fireplace for 14 days, two days after Twelfth Night, despite the efforts of Mr Brittan to get it to burn while his men made merry. He realised he had been duped but saw the funny side and rewarded the wily workers with a great supper and extra measures of ale.

The picturesque nature of Burwash, with its mixture of architecture spanning many centuries blending to make a main street of immense charm, has made it a favourite with visitors since long before Kipling's time. The older inhabitants will insist, albeit rather selfconsciously, that its correct pronunciation is Burrish, although this makes nonsense of the Rev John Coker Egerton's story about the village's name. This 19th century clergyman recounted that he was told, in all seriousness, by one of his parishioners that Burwash got its name from a dog. In Sussex Folk and Sussex Ways, he records the villager's explanation:

'When the Romans landed in Pevensey Bay, they had with them a dog called Bur; and after a while the dog got so bemired with the Sussex clay that he couldn't travel any further, so they washed him, and the place where they washed him was called 'Burwash'.'

It is another dog that haunts Spring Lane – in a most unnerving way. For the only part of this canine spirit to materialise is its

THE MILL,
BATEMANS

nose, sniffing in the darkness.

Captain John Leyland Feilden caused plenty of gossip and no doubt some fanciful rumours at the end of the last century. He lived at Rampyndene House and when his wife died in 1887 he refused to communicate with the rector, with whom he had fallen out. Instead he had her body embalmed and put in a small mausoleum in the garden. The Captain left the remains of his wife behind when he moved to the West Country and it was left to Henry Wemyss Feilden, when he moved in to Rampyndene, to have the body removed and interred in the churchyard.

The churchyard seems to have been rather a jolly sort of place a century or so ago, although in 1833 it was with shock that the Rev Horsefield noted that it 'was converted into a scene of youthful gaiety', and that games of every description were being played among the tombstones.

When it came to having a good time it was the blacksmiths who surpassed the other village tradesmen. Their big occasion was St Clement's Day (November 23) when the anvils were fired with a loud explosion and at least a half-holiday was kept to commemorate their patron saint. In the evening there was a 'Way-Goose', not a goose at all but a slap-up meal of roast pork with sage and onions, which all the village blacksmiths would attend. There used to be four here at the turn of the century, so presumably they let in a few outsiders to make a party of it.

A life-size dummy of Old Clem, stuffed with straw and complete with wig, beard and large clay pipe, was set up over the door of the inn to keep guard while the dinner was in progress. The oldest blacksmith present would start the proceedings with a toast to Vulcan, father of all smiths:

'Here's to Vulcan, as bold as a lion
A large shop and no iron
A big hearth and no coal
And a large pair of bellowses full of holes'

This was followed by singing and then the men refilled their glasses for the curious toast:

'True hearts and sound bottoms,
Checked shirts and leather aprons.'

The blacksmith returned to Burwash in 1985 after a break of nearly half-a-century when David Hedges set up business in the village. He had served a seven-year apprenticeship, learning all the aspects of the ancient craft, before spending 18 years in the police force. He had always wanted to return to being a blacksmith: 'Here at the end of the day I can see what I have achieved and know that the things I've made will probably last 200 odd years. That is a very nice feeling.'

Job satisfaction that must be the envy of many.

Buxted

This village underwent the sort of trauma that could so easily have shattered its identity. In the early years of the 19th century it abandoned its roots and moved to a new site half-a-mile away, leaving only its church in the middle of a private park.

The ancient settlement of Bloc Stede (Place of Beeches) was grouped around the Church of St Margaret the Queen, with a parsonage, an inn, a shop, a forge, stocks and a whipping post serving the cottages. Lord Liverpool became the owner of Buxted Place and wished to remove the village from its ancestral site so he could make his park larger and more exclusive. He offered to build new houses for the inhabitants anywhere in the parish if they would move, but not unnaturally, they turned him down.

Lord Liverpool then refused to carry out any repairs to the properties and they gradually fell into decay. The occupants were forced to leave, the houses were demolished and by 1836 there was nothing left to be seen of the old village. Only an old print in the church serves as a reminder of how things used to be.

Buxted Place itself has had a colourful career, surviving a disastrous fire in 1940 to later become a health farm and later still the

34

home of an Arab Sheik. The park is famous for its herd of deer and the large artificial lake which is home for many exotic birds.

The new settlement grew up with the railway line to become a thriving place, popular with commuters and with more than 20 clubs and organisations to keep the locals amused. A legacy of the old days lives on in Upper Totease, the clergyman's house which was rebuilt on its present site after the migration from the Park, with a mounting block still at its gates.

Of the scores of East Sussex villages that made a living out of the iron industry, Buxted demands a special claim on our attention for it was here that Ralf Hogge (or Huggett) perfected gun production in 1543 and became weapon maker by royal appointment:

> 'Master Huggett and his man John,
> They did cast the first cannon.'

The Hogge House, complete with a pig emblem and the date 1581, stands at the entrance of Buxted Park.

The village was also a centre of the silk-weaving industry, introduced and taught by refugee Flemish weavers, and for the growing of hops. They were still being produced at Howbourne Farm in the 1940s in fields that have now been swallowed up by the Manor Park Estate, part of the town of Uckfield but lying within Buxted parish. The oast houses survive as homes and the hops themselves grow wild in the hedgerows, an open invitation for people to put to the test the belief that the surest way to a good night's sleep is a pillow full of hops.

The unfortunate Nan Tuck was treated with less than civility by her contemporaries but won immortality in Buxted: 'Nan Tuck's Lane' proclaims the roadsign, though it was the scene of her terror and despair.

Old Nan, lived here in the 17th century, not a good time for old ladies who lived on their own. Through eccentricity or senility they stood the chance of being called witches and this was the accusation that fell upon Nan. She fled down the lane with her persecutors in full cry behind, disappearing into a wood never to be seen again according to one climax of the story, or to be found hanged in Tuck's Wood according to the sadder version. Nan's ghost is said to haunt the lane and when efforts were made to restock the wood with trees after the Great War there was one patch on which no sapling would ever grow...

A note in the parish register records the tragedy of Mary Relfe and James Atkinson who were due to be married in December 1742. Mary suddenly fell dangerously ill and despite the constant nursing of her fiance died one Sunday evening, James took to his bed, heartbroken and praying for death. He died the following Sunday at the same hour of the evening as Mary, and was buried beside her in the churchyard on the day they were to have been married.

Village idiots used to be an essential ingredient of the rural landscape. Buxted was no exception, but in George Watson they had an extraordinary character who made many people think again about this much-maligned segment of society. George was born in the village in 1785 and according to Hone's Table Book was 'ignorant in the extreme, and quite uneducated, not being able to read and write.' Yet he was a mathematical genius and could perform amazing feats of memory, solving the most difficult calculations and recalling the events of every day in his life from an early age – 'Upon being asked on what day a given day of the month occurred, he immediately names it, and also mentions where he was and what was the state of the weather.'

George's powers made him something of a celebrity and he was taken on several tours and proclaimed as a wonder. Mark Antony Lower, who said George's portrait depicted 'a middle-aged man, of gentle though half idiotic expression', wrote: 'I never saw George Watson but once: he was trudging up Malling Hill, eastward to Lewes, and his hat, considerably the worse for wear, was chalked all over with figures, apparently the result of some arithmetical feat he had recently performed, and which he had forgotten to rub out.'

Catsfield ✺

They had to wait a long time to ring the changes in the church of St Laurence – more than 200 years. The three church bells, the minimum needed for a peal, had been the centre of a mystery worthy of a whodunnit. One of them had been deliberately broken, by a person or persons unknown, sometime after 1724. Was it a midnight raid by the village blacksmith, upset by the ringers' refusal to peal for the wedding of his favourite daughter? Or was it the lord of the manor, who lived next door, driven to extremes by the inferior tolling of a bell described as 'lowering the tone of the place'?

The culprit will never be known. But in 1984 a £5,000 appeal in the village restored the bells, including the recasting of the cracked offender, and a fourth bell was donated by the Sussex Association of Change Ringers. St Laurence's two sound bells were among the oldest in the country, the tenor and the treble being cast in 1408 and 1418. One is embossed with *Sum rosa pulsata mundi Katerina vocata* (I am the clarion rose of the world and am called Katerina) and the other with *Dulcis sisto melis campana vocor Gabrielis* (I am the honey voiced bell called Gabriel).

It seems strange that this peaceful village, set in the rolling, wooded countryside on the road to the Conquest battlefield at Senlac, derives its name from the packs of wild cats which once prowled the area.

Catsfield is the last resting place of Thomas Brassey, the great railway engineer who settled in the village. This farmer's son began by constructing the Grand Junction in Britain and went on to build railways throughout the world including opening up the vastness of India, Canada and Australia.

It had a distinguished but ill-fated visitor in 1791. Princess de Lamballe, closest and most faithful friend of the doomed Marie Antoinette, brought several possessions of the French Queen to be deposited for safekeeping in the hands of Lady Gibbs at Catsfield Place. The Princess returned to Revolutionary France and was killed within a year of her mission to East Sussex.

Chailey 🦢

Beating the bounds of one of the largest parishes in the county requires more than a little ingenuity (not to mention stamina) from those taking part. Chailey's border stretches for 24 miles and the bound-beaters do the job as teams in relay, and treat it as a race to boot.

On foot, horseback, bicycle, canoe and even wheelbarrow the teams race against the clock each May raising money for good causes along the way in the form of sponsorship. Not surprisingly, it takes all day so the village makes the most of it with stalls and sideshows, a market, exhibitions and a barn dance in the evening to round off the occasion.

Chailey owes its size to the fact that it is really three villages in one: the old community, or Chailey Green, South Common and North Common. Chailey Green, gathered about the church, was once the hub of village life. Within living memory it boasted a village shop, a butcher's, a tailor's, a post office and a smithy. All these have now disappeared.

Nearby is Chailey Moat, better known in the past as The Parsonage, a centuries-old building surrounded, strangely, by a moat which is said to have been dug singlehanded by a parson in the reign of Queen Anne.

South Common is renowned today for its brickworks and in former times for its potteries. The Sussex clay belt runs through here and as early as 1740 Mr Norman established a business which remained in the hands of his descendants for 200 years. The kilns of the Chailey Potteries turned out bricks and tiles, drainpipes, flower pots and various terracotta articles.

North Common, a breezy nature reserve of gorse and bracken, is in total contrast to the more traditional rural landscape of its brother to the south. Its windmill has for generations been held to mark the exact centre of Sussex and nearby is the world-famous Chailey Heritage, home to some 160 physically handicapped residential and day pupils on three sites. This is a little community in its own right and was born in 1903 when Dame Grace Kimmins and her friend Alice Rennis gave a home at what had once been a workhouse to seven physically handicapped boys from London's East End.

Bogbean flourished on the common and was welcomed locally as a preventive of rheumatism, though it was regarded in many districts as a purifier of the blood. Gipsies were always eager to stop and gather many wild plants for medicinal purposes; juice from the berries of honeysuckle was valued as a cure for sore throats and the young shoots of broom were thought to be a useful antidote to kidney complaints.

Horsfield's *History of the Environs of Lewes,* published in 1827, devotes much space to one of Chailey's more eccentric characters. John Kember had all the characteristics of a miser or 'a plain and meanly dressed farmer' yet he spent vast sums on expensive books. Horsfield recorded that 'whilst some of his neighbours regarded him as a slave of avarice, others not more justly considered him as one of those whom much learning had rendered mad.'

He kept all his books neatly packed in boxes, taking them out occasionally to admire them, and also built up a sizeable collection of old maps and scientific instruments. After his death 'his books and philosophical apparatus were disposed of by auction in Lewes, and the competition was such as to turn to good account the taste of the worthy bibiomaniac.'

During the First World War the Rev T.H.L. Jellicoe listed the names of the village men serving in the Forces every month. In 1917 he wrote that Chailey was the 'first village to come under the East Sussex Health Association scheme for mothers schools', commenting that while nine soldiers died every hour in 1915, 12 babies died in Britain. In November 1918, when the national 'flu epidemic took its toll in Chailey, he wrote: 'I trust that the measures which I have adopted for supplying nourishment to the invalids may tend towards their recovery.'

It was young Basil Jellicoe, going to church for the first time, who let out a cry of alarm (or disappointment) when his father entered the pulpit: 'Why it's not God, only Daddy.'

The Five Bells inn took its name from the number of bells in the church, though it did not bother to change its name when a sixth was added in 1810. It was here that the Chailey Friendly Society, the oldest in the county, was formed and held its meetings in 1793. Its object was to raise 'a fund by subscription of the Members to be applied to their relief and maintenance in Sickness, Old Age and Infirmity also to the relief of their widows.'

The annual meeting of the society on June 4 was combined with a feast day which appears to have been celebrated by the whole parish with a day's holiday.

A landlord of The Swan in the last century was noted for his delicious stews, cooked in a great cauldron over the fire in the bar. One cold day a particularly fine smelling stew was being served up by the landlord when something strange appeared wrapped around the ladle. 'Well I'll be danged,' he said. 'I wondered where that ole sock had got to.'

Author and poet Siegfried Sassoon, 'Mad Jack' of the Great War, was frequently put up here when he went hunting with the Shiffner family at Bevern Bridge House. His recollections of The Swan formed pieces for his *Memoirs of a Foxhunting Man*.

Chalvington

Life was not easy for the people who lived in the 'Charnton' of feudal times. The lord of the manor did more than keep them in check – they were more or less imprisoned. He allowed none to pass the parish boundary without payment of a toll. Still, it worked both ways and discouraged visits from undesirable characters.

Behind the Yew Tree Inn is a cricket pitch reputed to be one of the oldest in the country. Matches have been played there for at least 200 years and in the last century the Sussex XI even used it for county games. England played here too in the 1970s, albeit the national ladies' team under Rachel Heyhoe-Flint who took on Ripe and Chalvington CC. The club had one of the first fatalities ever attributed to the switch from under-arm to over-arm bowling. An unfortunate batsman was struck on the knee by the ball (no pads in the first half of the 19th century) and died two weeks after having his leg amputated.

The fact that the name of the cricket team includes Chalvington's next door neighbour (they are practically semi-detached) is common in most things today, with the majority of activities taking place at the more populous Ripe. But little Chalvington retains its own identity where it can, and has a rare treasure in the church: Stained glass from the 13th century depicting, it is believed, St Thomas-a-Becket.

Chiddingly 🌿

A village which in its own humble way was said to resemble Rome, because the parish rests upon seven hills: Stone Hill, Gun Hill, Thunders Hill, Burgh Hill, Holmes Hill, Scrapers Hill and Pick Hill.

There was nothing humble about the Jefferay family, the old lords of the manor, whose pride was a byword. To stop their feet from getting soiled on the way to church they had a line of cheeses laid from their mansion to the church door to use as stepping stones. Some older residents will assure you that the story must be true because the impressive Jefferay monument in the church depicts two of the Sussex Marble figures standing upon round tablets like gigantic cheeses. The 18 feet high tomb is of Sir John Jefferay, Queen Elizabeth's Lord Chief Baron of the Exchequer, his wife and their daughter. Sadly, it has been much defaced, the theory being that somebody mistook the worthy Sir John for Judge Jeffreys of "Bloody Assize" infamy.

The Jefferays lived at Chiddingly Place and legend said a crock of gold was hidden in a gallery there, sat upon by an evil spirit guardian in the shape of a black hen. A yokel plucked up the courage to dislodge the hen and make off with the treasure but the bird knocked him senseless and flew in a fury through the great east window of the hall, pushing two iron bars out of shape on the way. The rustic never recovered from the experience; far from becoming rich he went out of his mind and had to be rocked in a cradle like a baby for the rest of his days.

Stone spires are a rarity in Sussex. There are only three and Chiddingly's is the best, a matter of pride which in recent years prompted the villagers to rally round and raise a massive sum for restoration work. It stands 130ft high, a gut-wrenching thought for vertigo sufferers but a fact that did not bother one adventurous local when the vane was regilded in the 1890s. He climbed to the top of the spire and balanced on his head on the apex to the excitement of the spectators on terra firma.

Chiddingly had its own drinking song, in rather dubious taste, which refers to the great estate of Peaks and of Perryland, just over the parish boundary:

'My daddy was a good ol' man,
He left me Peaks an' Perrylan',
But in the space of twent year,
I spent it all on gin and beer.'

There is singing in abundance here every year during the Chiddingly Festival, a week long celebration of the arts featuring everything from music and drama to painting and films. The locals even became film stars themselves, immortalised by local director Tony Penrose in his record of a year in the life of the village. His father was the late surrealist artist and art collector Sir Roland Penrose, who once had a painting turned down by the Royal Academy because it incorporated a poem with a swear word in it. Sir Roland successfully submitted another, which showed hands signalling a four-letter word in deaf-and-dumb sign language.

The great Sussex historian Mark Antony Lower was born in Chiddingly, where his father was the village schoolmaster. Dad was something of a writer himself and also a slave of the weed, a fact he laments in The Old Smoker's Six Reasons for Breaking his Pipe, which concludes:

'Farewell, broken pipe; King Tobacco, adieu!
No longer I bow in submission to you;
Those pleasures I seek that are lasting and free,
Which vainly are sought for in tyrants like thee;
I revoke my allegiance to thy petty reign;
Thy sceptre I've broken – I'll not smoke again!'

Cooksbridge

Word games and puzzles here. 'Coney' is an old Sussex word for a rabbit so it does not take a lot of stretching to turn Conyboro School into Rabbit Burrow School; and Shelley's Folly is the name of an 18th century mansion of Flemish bond brick. But should it not refer to the curious clump of pines on the adjacent hill, a natural 'folly' and a landmark for miles?

Even the name of the place has an unlikely story to account for its origin. Simon de Montfort's army stopped here on the march from Fletching to the Battle of Lewes in 1264 and the cooks served breakfast on the bridge.

Peppercorn rents do not seem as common in this material age as they used to be but at Cooksbridge The Malthouse is let to the parish council by Lord Monk Bretton at 1/- a year (still the old fashioned bob, not 5p) and a management committee is responsible for its maintenance.

The village once had its own brewery, supplying the local pubs. It has disappeared now, but still very much a part of the community after more than 100 years is McBeans Orchids, launched by Scotsman James Ure McBean with a single greenhouse in 1879. Today the firm is world famous for its steady stream of new varieties of delicate blooms and for the hundreds of prizes it has won.

Cross-In-Hand

The last working windmill in the county is the big eye-catcher, though its dominance high on the ridge has a rival in the new BBC television mast. The New Mill (Cross-in-Hand's old mill went out of action in 1903) has had a colourful past. It was built at Mount Ephraim in Framfield and moved to Cross-in-Hand in 1855, but Squire Huth did not approve of its proximity to his mansion and grounds, where local gossip suggested there were unseemly goings-on. So it was moved again a quarter-of-a-mile to its present site in 1868, carried on rollers hauled by a team of oxen.

The partnership of Newnham and Ashdown commenced grinding at the mill in 1868 and this family association continued until 1969 when a stock broke while the mill was working. But the sails may yet swing again. She is still owned by the Newnham family and a restoration programme is under way.

The English Place Name Society gives the earliest reference to the village as Cruce Manus in 1547, and the name is believed to be based on the legend that Crusaders assembled here before embarking for the Holy Land.

The village once had two fairs a year, on June 22nd and

November 19th, when the landlord of the Cross-in-Hand Hotel was expected to prepare a feast of roast beef and plum pudding with all the trimmings for the revellers. By tradition the fairs featured weight-lifting contests. This was always won by Strong John Saunders, a local miller who could lift 2cwt and died in 1835 at the age of 82.

A cottage industry that grew to greater things was established at Homestalls, in New Pond Hill, where George Foord lived with his wife Eliza and son 'Thomas Foord, aged 10, labourer.' Mrs Foord made ginger beer for the thirsty workmen out in the fields and young Thomas must have paid careful attention to mum's pop creation because in later life he made a successful business from it. He is recorded in Kelly's Directory of Sussex for the year 1882: 'Foord, Thomas. Manufacturer of ginger beer, lemonade, soda, seltzer, potash, ginger ale and other mineral waters for which he is famous.' He also found time to be a farmer and was parish surveyor at an annual salary of £10.

Another local delicacy was flead cakes (flead being pure lard from the pig's intestines) made by a baker called Tingley in Warren Lane. This was the recipe:

Flead pastry: 1 lb flead
               1lb plain flour
               pinch of salt
               ½ pint cold water
Method: Remove fat from membrane and rub one quarter of the flead into the flour. Add salt and water and mix to a smooth dough. Knead well. Roll out and use the method of incorporating the remaining fat as for flaky pastry. Shape and cut as desired.

Crowhurst

Yew trees are a standard feature in all old country churchyards, but here is the oldest in the county, 40 feet in circumference at the last count and so cracked with age that a grown man can climb inside. Testaments to its age range from 1,000 to 3,000 years. Certainly it must have been flourishing when William the Conqueror passed this way so it is not surprising that a story has grown up that the Normans hanged a Saxon from the tree because he refused to reveal details of Harold's approaching army.

The invaders left their mark on the place. The Domesday Book describes Crowhurst as 'devastated'.

Just below the church are the remains of an old manor house dating from the 13th century. Its builder, Walter de Scotney, chief steward to the Earl of Gloucester, came to a sticky end. He was accused of murdering his master and the Earl's brother. He was tried at Winchester and executed in 1259.

Crowhurst's old quarry is a haven for wildlife, supporting amongst other things a massive badger sett and burrowing bees. So the parish council reacted angrily when Battle Rifle Club proposed turning the site into an open air shooting range. The fauna won the day.

Godfrey and Ann Munn were licensees of The Plough Inn for 33 years until their retirement and introduced the famous Crowhurst Pumpkin Show. It hit a sticky patch when outsiders started to muscle in and the locals boycotted the event until finally a ban was put on visiting growers. Pumpkin fanciers compete in various classes, including heaviest, best shaped and ugliest. Cowman Tom Masters had perhaps the most ingenious growing method, the slurry tip at his farm producing monsters weighing in at more than 50lbs.

The Rev James Price Bacon-Phillips (1857-1938), letter writer extraordinary, was rector here for 28 years. He claimed to have had up to 9,000 letters printed in the Press and thousands more sent to newspapers on which he had not been able to check the fate of his missives. One of his key topics for such a prodigious outpouring was the way witnesses were bullied in court by opposing counsel.

Dallington 🌿

George Wagner, founder of the Penitents' Home in Brighton, waxed lyrical about the tranquility of the village when he was curate here in the 1840s. It is still a peaceful backwater which has not changed much since his day, so it is ironic that it has several close connections with warfare.

A roadside cross was erected by the mother of Flying Officer Peter Guerin Crofts who died after a dogfight over the village on September 28th, 1940. His Hurricane was badly hit and the young pilot baled out. His aircraft crashed at Earls Down, Red Pale, at precisely 1.55 pm and he landed at nearby South View Farm but died from his wounds. The cross, marking the spot where he fell, is tended by the Heathfield branch of the RAFA.

The late Captain 'Mac', Fleet Street cartoonist, camouflage expert and war hero, lived in Dallington for 45 years. He was George Douglas Machin, affectionately known locally as a charming if eccentric character. Residents would see him walking along the road, oblivious to his surroundings, pulling his folio of drawings behind him on wheels, often wearing enormous gumboots. He served as a balloon observer in the First World War, with the hazardous job of floating above enemy lines to plot their positions, and was awarded the Distinguished Flying Cross. He found fame as a cartoonist for his work on *Blighty,* the soldiers' newspaper. His output was prolific throughout his life and

DALLINGTON.

the signature 'Mac' appeared on drawings in scores of publications.

Herrings Place was the big house of the village until it burned down in 1803, and two daughters from the manor were married to generals: Mary Randoll to Lt Gen John Mackenzie (who had a distingushed career in the Marines) and Jane Crawford to Lt Col Donald MacDonald (who rose to the rank of Brigadier while serving in America). They are all buried at Dallington.

There is a strong local tradition that a man from the village fought with General George Custer at the Battle of the Little Bighorn in 1876. Such an idea is not so far-fetched as many former British Army cavalrymen swelled the ranks of the US Cavalry during the indian wars. Unfortunately, nobody can now put a name to the recruit from East Sussex who died at the hands of the Sioux in Custer's Last Stand at Greasy Grass.

When the Ashburnham family bought the Herrings Estate in 1801 they acquired (among other things) the Herrings pew in Dallington church. There was a long drawn-out court case between the Ashburnhams, who wanted to preserve the pew, and the Church authorities, who wanted it destroyed to make way for general restoration. The case became too costly for the family to continue and 'improvements' went ahead which were generally held to be disastrous in the old building.

Village traditions are not necessarily old. Over the past 30 or so years the older folk here have enjoyed a Christmas party organised for them by the Keeley family. Mrs Mabel Keeley, affectionately known to the children as Nanny Keeley, started it all and with her death in 1981 it was feared the tradition might not continue, but her husband Percy, his sons and friends have continued to provide Dallington's elderly and those living alone with a party which has become a memorial to the lady who began it.

Danehill 🦢

No marauding Danes here, but certainly a hill from which the village enjoys some of the finest views in the county. The name is a corruption of 'Den' meaning an enclosure on the forest.

47

There has been a settlement on the old East Grinstead to Lewes turnpike for centuries, but the parish is a modern one, formed in 1898 from chunks of Fletching and Horsted Keynes.

Richard Tamplin was born here at the end of the 18th century. He came from a family of mercers and his father died in debt, but Tamplin built-up one of the largest breweries in Sussex and though it has long since been absorbed by one of the national giants the name lives on to this day. Tamplin's first brewery at Southwick was destroyed by fire in 1811 and he made a fresh start at the appropriately named Phoenix Brewery in Brighton. He was the right man in the right place at the right time as Brighton was just about to take off as a seaside resort and there were a growing number of thirsts to be quenched.

They are fond of the past in Danehill and the village's historical society has more than 120 members. The first president of the society was 90-year-old Dame Margery Corbett Ashby, an early leader of the women's rights movement who was born in the village in 1882. At the age of 19 her interest in politics led her to become national secretary of the Constitutional Suffrage Movement, and in 1924 she was elected president of the International Alliance of Women. She was one of the United Kingdom delegates at the disarmament conference in Geneva in 1932. When she died in 1981 the Historical Society published a commemorative book on her life.

Hidden away on the forest at Chelwood Gate is a memorial to President John F. Kennedy. Five months before his assassination in 1963, he came here for talks with Prime Minister Harold Macmillan (now Lord Stockton) who lives at Birchgrove.

Denton 🦢

The late Ralph Reader, of *Gang Show* fame, grew up here and that has meant a singular honour for the local Scout troop who go by the exalted title of the 2nd Denton and South Heighton (Ralph Reader's Own).

The church, the small manor house, a handful of flint cottages and The Flying Fish Inn are all that remain of the old village which has been engulfed by suburbia, though there are some old timers who remember when there used to be a dairy at the back of the pub and a spring at the side where the local farmers used to take their cattle to drink.

The church, where Parson Bedford used to preach for 64 years, was re-consecrated after the English Civil War because the Parliamentarian soldiers billeted here used the building as a stable.

The Dickers

In June 1677 the treasurer of the Earl of Sussex recorded a successful sporting bet by his master and inadvertently put Dicker into the record books. The wager dutifully put down on paper was: 'Paid to my lord when his lordship went to the creckitt match at ye Dicker 03.00.0' (the princely sum, in those days, of £3).

No details of this match of long ago survive, but it proved that cricket flourished in the village and is one of the earliest recorded encounters in the history of the game. It has been played in Dicker ever since and the 300th anniversary was celebrated in suitable style when the local lads entertained teams from the MCC and Sussex County Cricket Club. In 1880 Luther Page was captain of the side, 'taking many wickets with his slow tweekers', and his descendants have played for the village ever since.

President of Dicker Cricket Club in the early years of the century was Horatio Bottomley, one of the most colourful characters of his era. There are still some old folks who remember with affection Upper Dicker's squire – Bottomley the MP, the financial wizard, the brilliant orator, womaniser and mammoth swindler. He is recalled by them as a kind and generous man who built many of the comfortable cottages, livened-up country life with lavish parties, knew everyone by name and made patriotic speeches at the village school. Bottomley, the orphan who made a fortune through newspapers and publishing, built himself a mansion at Upper Dicker where he had the only telephone in the parish but allowed everyone to use it. Fraudulent Australian gold boom companies, rigged competitions and lotteries were his undoing and in 1922 he appeared at the Old Bailey on 24 fraud counts and was jailed for seven years. He came out of prison a broken man and died, bankrupt, in 1933. The Dicker, the mansion home of his heyday and declining years, is now a school.

At Upper Dicker can be found Michelham Priory, the loveliest bit of the river Cuckmere, founded in 1229 for Augustinian Canons on an island surrounded by a moat. Parts of the priory buildings, including the church, were destroyed in the Dissolution in 1536 and the remaining buildings formed the nucleus of a Tudor house. It was given to the Sussex Archaeological Society in 1959. Like all good priories, it is said to be haunted by the ghost of a monk.

Lower Dicker, with Sussex perversity, lies a mile or so to the north, a straggling place torn in half by the busy A22. Old postcards show it to have been a peaceful place in earlier days and it was famous for its clay flowerpots as the local hostelry, The Potter's Arms, testifies.

Ditchling 🦥

Ditchling people have had a lot to put up with down the years. There was the witch who lived out on the Common in a house called Jack o'Spades who held up work on the farms by stopping waggons as they rolled past. Presumably she was helped by a couple of muscular and devoted henchmen.

Like all witches, she had the power to transform herself into a hare. One night the waggoners decided to get their revenge and lay in wait for her with dogs. The next day the witch summoned assistance in binding up a bite on the leg where one of the dogs had caught her as she jumped through the window in hare form.

Then there were the witch hounds which roamed by night on the highest point in East Sussex at Ditchling Beacon. This supernatural pack was credited with unpleasant but unspecified powers, and as late as 1935 it was reported that their baying had been heard on the Downs.

Closer to home was the ghost that haunted the cellars of one of the village shops, and the very real chance of being swallowed-up by the ground: There are a variety of village stories of the earth suddenly giving way and people tumbling into deep holes which were old forgotten wells, of which Ditchling had more than its

50

fair share.

Locals were not the only ones to endure trial and tribulation. Rivalry between Ditchling and its neighbour Keymer was so fierce and the desire to keep the two villages apart so strong that many bitter struggles were fought on the fields that separate them. Within living memory a Keymer youth who came courting a Ditchling girl risked being ducked in the water butt outside The Bull Inn or even worse being tossed into the village pond.

Happily for ardent suitors who wanted to stay dry the revision of the county boundary put Keymer over the border in West Sussex and ensured that never the twain would meet.

Ditchling liked to be known as a 'royal and ancient town', an exalted title with slender links. The Manor of Ditchling was the property of King Alfred and it later belonged to Edward the Confessor. Edward II kept a stud of horses here when he was Prince of Wales for hunting in the royal park and in 1312 he gave permission for a weekly market to be held on Tuesdays. He also granted a charter for a fair on the Eve, Feast and Morrow of St Margaret of Antioch, now long disappeared and forgotten but replaced by the celebrated Ditchling Gooseberry and Copper Kettle Fair which has been held in the Star Field since 1822.

It began life with the formation of Ditchling Horticultural Society and gloried in the full title of Gooseberry and Currant Show, Stoolball Match and Kettle Feast. In the first year prizes were offered for the best faggot stack, the cleanest cottage and the best pig in a sty. The copper kettle was the prize for the heaviest pint of gooseberries.

Ditchling's superb setting under the hills has made it a popular place with the famous. They range from artists like Sir Frank Brangwyn, the sculptor Eric Gill, poetess Mrs Meynell and actress Dame Ellen Terry. In our own times Dame Vera Lynn and cartoonist Rowland Emmett have been drawn to the place.

The calligrapher Edward Johnston came in 1912 and displayed new talents for transforming everyday objects into little works of art, like making a miniature saucepan out of a tobacco tin and cooking in it new potatoes the size of peas. His friend Gerard Meynell, founder of the Westminster Press, was stretching things a bit when he sent Johnston two sardine tins with a note stating 'please make me a motor bicycle and a telescope.'

The church choir were smugglers to a man 200 years ago and the Common was a notorious haunt of thieves, so in the face of this lawlessness in the days before 'peelers' there was formed a remarkable society of amateur policemen. The Ditchling Society consisted of property owners and one of the principal objects was to raise funds for 'prosecuting thieves, etc.' It was established in 1784 and flourished until at least 1834 with an annual meeting at The Bull where, according to the rules, dinner was to be on the table at two o'clock in the afternoon and each member was to pay 'three shillings to defray the expenses thereof.'

Today's upholders of the law would be round like a shot to the old toll house to the north of the village, where in the 18th century there lived an old lady whose recreation was smoking opium, the local shop feeding her addiction with no restriction on sales in those days.

The simplicity of the rustic natives seems to have been given more attention by writers than other villages. Like the old lady from Ditchling in the early years of the last century who was about to travel to London for the first time in her life from a place where the one excitement to disturb a dog asleep at the crossways would be the rattling of a coach down the High Street. Her friends asked what kind of place she expected the great metropolis to be.

'I cannot exactly tell,' she said. 'But I reckon it must be very like the busy end of Ditchling High Street.'

Or the man who was reading aloud the notice of the death of a resident: 'The deceased (which the yokel pronounced diseased) came to Ditchling a decade (decayed) back'. All was revealed to the reader: 'Ah. I rac'n'd 'eed got summat a matter wid 'im, but I did'n allow as 'twer 'is back.'

Old Tom Weller, the wooden-legged cattle tender on Ditchling Common, swore by a pair of mole's feet as a cure for toothache. He apparently sold scores of them at sixpence a pair. It sounds nearly as unpleasant as sitting in the dentist's chair.

East Chiltington 🌿

One character stands out vividly in the landscape of a history which spans nearly 1,000 years. Susannah Stacey, better known as

Grandma, was by any measure a remarkable woman – cook and counsellor, friend to the poor and the sick, a healer through strange herbal potions. She was a curious mixture of well-bred Victorian lady and white witch.

The daughter of a wealthy Surrey family, she ran away at the age of 19 to marry farmer Mr William Stacey, a widower with five children, and her home became East Chiltington's Stantons Farm. The rest of her life seems to have been devoted to the people of the hamlet and to the poor who would call at her door. Stantons became a place of pilgrimage for those who were troubled in mind or body and Grandma's advice and medicines were never denied them.

She created a herb garden famous throughout the county and the products of her stills would be sought after by doctors for miles around. She had a herbal remedy for every human ailment from lumbago to deafness and was just as famous for her cures of domestic animals. Several outbreaks of the dreaded foot and mouth disease in cattle were believed to have been thwarted by her powers, and she could soothe a frenzied horse or pain-wracked dog by the touch of her hand or the sound of her voice.

Entertainment must have been on a lavish scale during the reign of the wise woman of Stantons (always addressed by her husband as 'ma'am') and many of her countless notes of household 'receipts' have survived. Not many 20th century households could budget for culinary creations which require the pounded flowers of a peck of cowslips, pickled nasturtium leaves or the copious quantities of wine and spirits often involved.

Some of the ingredients may have been unusual, but the result was no doubt delicious. This was Grandma's recipe for Herb Pie:

'Pick two handfuls of parsley, half the quantity of spinach, two lettuces, mustard and cresses, a few leaves of burridge, and white beet leaves; wash and boil them a little; drain, press out the water; cut them small; mix and lay them in a dish, sprinkled with salt. Mix a batter with flour, two eggs well beaten, a pint of cream, and half a pint of milk, and pour it on to the herbs; cover with a good crust, and bake it.'

Or how about this fox-glove concoction as a cure for deafness:

'Bruise in a marble mortar, the flowers, leaves and stalks of fresh fox-glove; mix the juice with double the quantity of brandy, and keep it for use. The herb flowers in June, and the juice will thus keep good till the return of that season. The method of using it is to drop one drop in the ear every night, and then moisten a bit of lint with a little of the juice, put it also in the ear, and take it out next morning till the cure be completed.'

Grandma died in 1893, but continued to be a source of help from beyond the grave. During her lifetime she had planted banks of belladonna, or deadly nightshade, in Cripps Plantation on the Downs above East Chiltington. As lethal as the name suggests if the plant is swallowed, she cultivated it for making belladonna plasters to ease various pains such as lumbago. The First World War brought a tremendous demand for the plant, its external application causing dilation of the pupils of the eyes making examinations and operations easier, and Grandma's flourishing wild garden of the stuff found a new role.

The village, clustered around its 12th century church, has not changed much since Grandma's era. The hovels which were home to many of her patients have gone and the village school is now a private house (though the owners have not removed the Victorian sense of propriety with seperate sections for boys and girls still clearly marked on the walls).

The Jolly Sportsman has undergone something of an identity crisis over the years. What does the name conjure-up? The painters of the pub sign have over the years depicted a jovial old gentleman, pockets bulging with game; another aged yokel lustfully pursuing a girl who looked old enough to be his great-granddaughter; and latterly a jockey obviously mounted on a winner.

East Dean

The Tiger Inn, eye-catcher of the oldest part of the village which lies on the seaward side of the Eastbourne road, probably got its name by error. It was taken from the Bardolf coat of arms which depicts a leopard. This could have been an understandable mistake 400 years ago when a simple innkeeper would never have seen either beast.

There are firemarks above the doors of two cottages next to the shop. These were the emblem of the insurance company and the policy number so the company's fire fighters could tell at a glance whether a blazing house was insured with them. Presumably if it was not they left it to burn!

The bow-fronted house called Dipperies was built by James Dippery on ill-gotten gains. This 18th century gentleman smuggler amassed a fortune from his illicit trading until one day he was caught red-handed by the Excise men and sent with his cronies for trial. Dippery turned King's evidence, was instrumental in sending his old confederates to Botany Bay for the rest of their natural lives and then settled down a free man to build his house and make the most of the loot.

If the sea played its part in making men like Mr Dippery rich it was also the downfall of many mariners on the treacherous coastline just south of East Dean, which had an appalling record of shipwrecks.

Parson Jonathan Darby, vicar here from 1715-1728, hollowed out a room in the face of the cliff at Belle Tout, well above the high-tide line, and constructed a sloping tunnel and steps to lead up to it from the beach. He would shine a light from his cavern out to sea on stormy nights and wait for any sailors struggling to make their way up to his sanctuary. 'Parson Darby's Hole' disappeared because of coast erosion at about the same time as the Belle Tout lighthouse went up in 1831.

Beachcombing for the cargoes of the wrecks must have been a profitable pastime for the village and a 16th century document indicates that a court of inquiry was held to establish what each man had taken when a ship laden with wine came to grief on the parish foreshore.

Still standing in the village is the first cable office connecting Britain with the continent. Its wires were carried on telegraph poles over the Downs to connect with the under-sea cable at Birling Gap.

The church registers tell the eerie story of Agnes and Joan Payne, who were buried here in 1796. Agnes was taken ill and lay speechless for 24 hours before suddenly crying out to her sister to make ready to come, as she could not go without her. Joan was in good health but within half-an-hour she too became ill, growing worse overnight as Agnes continued to call for her to come. The two sisters died together in the morning. The story's accuracy was vouched for by the vicar and three churchwardens.

Birling Manor was the home of the Gurneys and when Juliana Gurney married William Bardolf in 1257 the house was probably part of her marriage portion. A decade later William Bardolf was granted a licence from the King to hold a weekly market and an annual fair at East Dean. The fair, held on the feast day of St Simon and St Jude, patron saints of the parish church, continued until the dawn of the present century.

THE TIGER INN
EAST DEAN

56

The Bardolf family may have had the knack of marrying rich young heiresses but also the fatal flaw of backing the wrong side. Hugh Bardolf, son of William and Juliana, was adviser to the ill-fated King John and Lord Thomas Bardolf (who appears in Shakespeare's Henry IV) took part in the Earl of Northumberland's revolt against Henry IV, was wounded in battle and died soon afterwards. In 1406 he was posthumously dishonoured in Parliament and his lands forfeited to the Crown.

Birling was later granted back to the family, only to be finally lost in 1461 because Lord William Bardolf fought for the Lancastrians against Edward IV.

A branch of a family that had better luck with royalty lived at Pendrills, the village's old laundry where the washing was once hung out on the hill behind to dry. It was the home of the descendants of the Pendrell brothers who hid Charles II in the oak tree at Boscobel and were richly rewarded at the Reformation when the King granted the family a pension of £100 a year in perpetuity.

East Guldeford

Follow the straight road east of Rye for a mile or so across the flatlands and you come to the last village in Sussex, more a part of the so-called sixth continent of the world, Romney Marsh. This cluster of cottages, a farm or two and a barn-like church is the embryonic 'brother' of a city, for Guildford in Surrey and this hamlet share a common bond in Sir Richard Guldeford. His family took their name originally from Guildford and he it was who gave the church to East Guldeford (pronounced Gilford, just to add to the confusion).

The church was built of brick in 1505 and underwent a careful restoration in the mid 1970s which retained all its character and charm.

Sir Richard also built the sea wall that protects the parish today and drained the area to transform it from a sea-washed marsh to fine farming land. His work here done, he set off on a pilgrimage to the Holy Land.

They must have been stoic characters in the past to have settled down to life in this lonely, windswept corner. But there were lighter moments. Arthur Beckett, in *The Wonderful Weald,* recounts the tale of the clergyman, a stranger to the district, who undertook the service at the church one Sunday morning. Before the service began the parish clerk asked him if he would mind 'praiching' in the reading desk, 'for my old hen has made her nest in the pulpit, and, as she is sitting, I shouldn't like to have her disturbed.'

East Hoathly

A plaque on the wall of one of the cottages beside the busy main road marks the old home of the village's most famous son. He was Thomas Turner (1729-1789), the village's Samuel Pepys whose candid diaries bring the atmosphere of his age vividly alive and leave the reader sometimes despairing of the author.

Turner, who among other things was village schoolmaster, undertaker and draper, fought a constant battle between piety and the demon drink. In 11 years he filled more than 100 books with a full and sincere account of his lapses and repentances. The lapses were frequent, with many furious drinking bouts in the village and further afield, breaking his own 'Rules of Proper Regimen' which were 'never to drink more than four glasses of strong beer. If there is either wine or punch never on any terms of persuasion to drink more than eight glasses. I will always go to bed at or before ten'.

It was on his bed one memorable morning that Turner was goaded by a group of friends (including the parson) to put on his wife's petticoats and dance without shoes and stockings for the amusement of the drunken visitors, though there is a more typical entry for February 2, 1758: 'We supped at Mr Fuller's and spent the evening with a great deal of mirth, till between one and two. Tho. Fuller brought my wife home upon his back. I cannot say I came home sober, though I was far from being bad company. I think we spent the evening with a great deal of pleasure.'

In addition to problems with the bottle Turner seems to have had problems with his wife, Peggy Slater, though after her death she is always referred to in his diary in the most reverent terms. His intimate disclosures cease with his second marriage, to Molly Hicks (though not before revealing that she was rather plain).

The 'Sussex Cannibal' lived in East Hoathly. He was the Cavalier Colonel Sir Thomas Lunsford, a giant of a man who was said to dine on children (he supposedly went about with infant limbs in his pocket by way of mid-meal snacks). Whatever his gruesome reputation, it was for killing deer in the park of Sir Thomas Pelham that the colonel was tried in 1632 and for a murderous assault upon its owner when he took a pot shot at him outside the church. The trail of the bullet can still be seen on the stonework on the south side of the west door. The colonel seems to have escaped with a hefty fine and in 1649 he 'sold all he had' and emigrated with his family to Virginia.

One of the numerous Sussex homes of the Pelhams was Halland Place, which lay on the parish boundary between East Hoathly and Laughton. When one of the family's old retainers fell into pauperism the two parishes went to Law to decide which would have to foot the bill for his claim for relief. The pauper had spent most of his life at Halland Place but a survey revealed that his bed stood over the parish boundary. The Law duly decided that East Hoathly should have to pay for his shelter and sustenance because his head had lain in the parish when he was asleep.

A village parson of the old days was a renowned scruff, with a shirt that was always hanging out and ragged breeches. A bountiful lady of the village found his sartorial style particularly offensive and so bequeathed him one pair of breeches a year. She also presented his successors with an area of glebe and woodland, the income from which was to be devoted to a new pair of breeches for the parish parson. The site is still known as Breeches Wood.

In the church is a dainty piece of Norman art which was once thrown out as rubbish. The pillar piscina, with zigzag decoration on the shaft, was dug up in the churchyard during restoration work in the 19th century and restored to its proper place.

The village has found it difficult to come to terms with the effects of the motor car. With a 90 degree bend in the heart of the old community, it was simply not built to cope with the hordes of summer day trippers eating up the miles to the coast at Eastbourne. Relief is in sight in the shape of a bypass, though there has been much argument and controversy over which route it should take.

Eridge

The closure of village schools on economic grounds has become an unpleasant fact of country life. When Eridge school closed its doors for the last time in 1979 after 102 years they at least went out in style. A farewell concert featured the children performing the Song of Eridge, written by teacher Mrs Joan McHutchison, which ended:

> 'Now they tell us we're closing,
> We're sad at the thought.
> So you'll just have the echoes
> The old school has caught.'

Before the concert began a furniture van arrived sent by East Sussex County Council, which had ordered the closure, to take away the school piano. The men were made to wait until the proceedings were over.

The crest of the Nevill family, Earls and Marquesses of Abergavenny, adorns many of the village houses for Eridge Park is the seat of this leading Sussex family. Even the pub is called The Nevill Crest and Gun. They have owned Eridge since at least 1300 and Queen Elizabeth I stayed at a shooting lodge here in 1573.

The house was remodelled into a vast Gothic castle by the Second Earl in 1810, who renamed it Eridge Castle and made it his chief residence instead of Kidbrooke Park, near East Grinstead. It once had 70 miles of rides and drives. The castle was demolished in 1938 and the modern house which replaced it has since been reduced to one third of its original size and is now known by its original name of Eridge Park.

There is a barn in the parish which is haunted by a maid from the big house. She hanged herself from a beam in the barn in the Victorian age when suicide was preferable to disgrace for an unmarried girl who became pregnant.

There must have been considerable alarm on the estate one November day in 1830 when the 'Swing Riots' were breaking out. A mob of agricultural workers marched on the castle intending to besiege it in their demand for higher wages. But they were poorly organised and the leaders were arrested: James Poulter, a Frant baker accused of inciting the trouble in the first place, was imprisoned for two months. He was lucky for in East Sussex as a whole nine men were sentenced to death and 457 were transported.

They make good use of the rugged terrain and rocky outcrops at Eridge where there is an outdoor pursuits centre. Among other things you can learn mountaineering and canoeing.

Etchingham ✻

Legend said that a great bell lay at the bottom of the moat surrounding the village church, and that it would never be seen until six yoke of white oxen were brought to drag it up. But the passage of time has punctured this romantic tale like so many others. The moat has gone and no bell has ever surfaced.

The church is an arresting sight in itself with its massive central tower and is generally held to be the finest example of Decorated work in the county. It has other claims to fame: The oldest dated brass in Sussex depicting its builder in 1366, William de Echyngham; the oldest weather vane in the country; and the largest series of misericords in Sussex apart from those at Chichester Cathedral. Misericords were ledges under tip-up stalls designed to offer a little comfort to those who could not stand throughout the long medieval services. Etchingham has an unusually carved one which shows a fox preaching to geese. The church also has a monument to Henry Corbould, the designer of the 'Penny Black', the world's first postage stamp introduced in 1840. The de Echynghams dominated the area for many years, a family loyal always to the King and usually held in high esteem by him. Our present Queen is descended (through the Bowes-Lyon branch of her family) from Anne de Echyngham.

The family's great manor house has disappeared without trace, but there are numerous other interesting houses in the village, particularly King's Lodge where the unfortunate King John of France lived in exile after his capture at the Battle of Poitiers in 1356. Another is Court Lodge with its priest hole and exposed beams which are said to come from ships of the Spanish Armada sunk in Rye Harbour in 1558.

Nature can still be hard on the people who live at the point where the rivers Dudwell and Rother unite, the low-lying nature of the parish making it a frequent victim of winter flooding. But their feet have not become webbed to make getting around easier, despite what some might tell you.

Horses have long since ceased to be the powerhouse of the farm but they are staging a remarkable revival in this village where Brenda and John Lavis believe they still have a useful role to play in the country. The couple are bringing back the working horses of the old days through the Sussex Shires, based at 17th century Haremere Hall, where horses are bred and advice given on the different jobs they can do. These gentle giants have become one of the fastest growing tourist attractions in the area, drawing more than 46,000 visitors in 1984.

Ewhurst Green

Living in a picture postcard community can have its drawbacks. There is no shop, no post office and no village hall. For a while there was no pub, either, until Tina Rainbow and her partner Richard Hayward re-opened The White Dog Inn in 1985 – and in doing so she became the youngest licensee in the country at 19 years of age.

The 17th century establishment used to be called The Castle Inn until the late 1960s when the name was changed to avoid confusion with the pub of the same name just up the road at Bodiam. The fact that the licensees Paul and Pauline Collins had a pet dog which happened to be white seems to have influenced their choice.

The village has a recreation ground to be proud of today, though a decade ago it was little more than a farm field. It was left to the parish as a recreation ground by Lieutenant A. Herdman who was killed in the First World War, but after the closure of the village school the field went out of use and was let for grazing every year by the parish council. A petition signed by most residents brought about a return to the use for which it was intended.

Ewhurst folk were either particularly prosperous or particularly generous three centuries ago. After the Great Fire of London in 1666 they contributed 'seven shillings and eightpence for the relief of the poor of St Bartholomew Exchange and St Bene't Fink of London for their losses sustained by the fire'. A humane gesture for a remote community whose inhabitants had probably never been to London.

The church has a spire with a distinct kink in it, and in the record books can be found Miss Fight-The-Good-Fight-Of-Faith White. Hopefully her Puritan parents allowed her to be known by a name which was less of a mouthful, on weekdays at least.

Fairlight 🦋

A country park of unspoilt sandstone cliffs, broken by gorse and tree-covered glens tumbling down to the sea, stretches for five miles from Fairlight to Hastings. A lofty spot where at one time you could see 70 Martello towers, 66 churches, 40 windmills, five castles, and three bays.

In the churchyard is buried Thomas Attwood Walmisley (1814-1856), who became Professor of Music at Cambridge at the tender age of 22 and so improved the internal workings of the organ at Trinity that the college boasted its instrument was unique and would be an object of curiosity for years to come. He was a friend of Mendelssohn, editing several of the composer's compositions and apparently unabashed when the great man roundly condemned one of Walmisley's own symphonies.

A wreck under the cliffs here in the last century left bodies, fragments of pianofortes and casks of spirits lying on the shore. There was only one survivor, a lad who was found clinging to the rocks, raving mad. News of the disaster sent crowds of men rushing to the beach to tap the casks, Coventry Patmore recording with disgust that some of them literally drank themselves to death and lay with other corpses on the beach. Patmore placed the blame for this excessive behaviour in the midst of a tragedy on the fishermen of Hastings. No doubt the good people of Fairlight did as well.

Fairwarp 🐑

'House sheep', kept by cottagers principally for ewe milk, were 300 years ago as commonplace as the 'house cow' and later the 'house pig.' As herds of dairy cattle were built up, so sheep rearing turned more towards the production of meat and wool.

Here farmer Mark Hardy has successfully turned back the clock and pioneered the reintroduction of sheep milk to Britain. The product of his mixed herd of Sussex High Weald Dairy Sheep is pure white, rich in calcium and protein, naturally sweet and without the 'taint' associated with goat milk.

It is a business far removed from the old time ways of earning a crust in this village on the edge of Ashdown Forest. There were ironworks here from Roman times, then charcoal-burning, hop growing and nursery gardening on land reclaimed from the forest enjoyed boom days. There is still a living to be made from the forest today in the form of Christmas wreaths for which there is an abundance of natural materials.

Fords are a rarity these days. Fairwarp has one and is proud of it. So much so that when East Sussex County Council channelled the water to run under the road there was such an outcry among the locals that council workmen had to come back and restore the stream to its original course across the lane.

Brooding over the forest uplands at Duddleswell are the radio masts of the Foreign Office's diplomatic wireless service station by which London stays in touch with Britain's embassies around the globe. A series of mounds found here puzzled archaeologists until it was established that they were part of the field kitchens that served the 12 army regiments camped here in 1793.

Nature reserves do not come much smaller than that established in the village in 1981. The attractive spread of a mere 8½ acres is under the care of a volunteer warden.

Every year the local youngsters smarten up their rabbits, cats and dogs and take them along to the village hall for the annual

pet show. The rules are strict though: no snakes and no pet larger than a goat.

Falmer

People still have bitter sweet recollections of Fiery Fred, the terror of Falmer Pond. Fred was a swan with a mean streak who took to attacking visitors to his watery domain, chasing after them with a great flapping of wings and snapping at their ankles with his beak.

There were complaints, and the question of what to do to curb the bird's belligerent character was discussed by the parish council in the early 1970s. Members decided drastic steps would have to be taken before somebody was seriously injured, so it was decreed that Fred should be banished from the village. He was transported to a new, more remote pond near Poynings in West Sussex where he would have fewer opportunities to take out his foul temper on humans. By all accounts Fiery Fred simmered down, raised a family and lived happily ever after. Today's pond residents are a much tamer bunch: ducks, geese and a collection of seagulls who prefer it to the beach at Brighton.

It was the pond, once 16 feet deep and positively dangerous until it was partly filled in, that gave the village its name (though locals are quick to point out that the early origins were Faelmere, not Foul).

War Memorials come in all shapes and sizes, but there are not many in the county that come in the form of a horse trough. It now serves as a flower bed and when the inscription stone became badly worn local craftsman Owen Williams sculpted a new one for a re-dedication service in May, 1985.

This is a divided village, not in a social sense but physically. Road widening in the 1970s meant the demolition of six cottages and now the busy A27 cuts right through the community with only a pedestrian bridge to span the chasm. It was not a popular project when work began, but residents have come to terms with progress and will admit that pedestrians are at least safer now than they were in the old days.

Rapid change has become a way of life here, the road widening being preceded by the construction of Brighton Polytechnic and Sussex University on Falmer's doorstep.

The journalist Godfrey Winn, who had a regular column in The Daily Mirror for many years, lived in the Mill House. It was more than just a bolt-hole in the country to him; he took an active part in community life, and one particular fete he organised to raise money for the church is still talked about. He died here in 1971.

Firle

Even if you have never been here the chances are that you have seen it, however unconsciously. The old houses and narrow village street are a favourite with television and film crews seeking an authentic backdrop for period pieces.

Technically its full name is West Firle, but a look at the map will not find you an East, or a North and South for that matter. There was an East Firle once, a vanished village known by the alternative name of Heighton St Clere. When Eleanor St Clere married John Gage of Cirencester in the early 15th century she brought her estates with her and these were augmented by the marriage of their son William in 1472 to Agnes Bolney, co-heiress of the manor of Firle, where the Gage family have lived ever since. Their home down the centuries has been Firle Place, a mellow mansion regularly open to the public and containing a superb collection of furniture and works of art.

The influence of the Gage dynasty has helped to make Firle special: Remote beneath the hills and its famous 718ft beacon, unspoilt and almost feudal in nature. The church is full of memorials to them; the village reading room was given by public subscription in 1913 in honour of the then Viscount and bears the initial 'G' and a coronet over the door; even the pub belongs to the Gages.

The family's fame as the friends of royalty, as distinguished soldiers, sailors and statemen, should not blind us to the fact that the greengage was first grown in England at Firle Place, intro-duced by the botanical traveller Thomas Gage.

Another Thomas Gage was Commander-in-chief of the British forces in America at the outbreak of the War of Independence which followed his skirmish at Lexington in April 1775. Two months later he fought and lost the Battle of Bunker's Hill and resigned.

Change comes slowly in Firle and it was a wrench for the regu-lars in 1985 when the Hafflett family ended their 77-year link with The Ram Inn. The outgoing tenants were George Hafflett and his wife Mary, whose grandfather and then mother had run the old inn since 1908. The couple took a family heirloom with them – the pub cash till so antiquated that it was capable of giving change for a sovereign!

The strange tale of the 'phenomenon in the sky' made the vil-lage the focus of world attention during the Second World War. Several people were witness to the vision of the crucified Christ appearing in the sky surrounded by angels, and a Mrs Steer was able to tell a *Southern Weekly News* reporter: 'I happened to go outside my back door and noticed a white streak or road across the sky. Then gradually I saw a cross appear, standing upright, with Christ upon it. Shortly afterwards there were six angels on each side of Him. It quite frightened me at first. I felt quite ill and I called my neighbour to look at it.'

Mrs Steer said the figure of Christ had the head drooping to one side: 'I could see the nails in His feet and in His hands, and the angels were so plain I could see their fingers and their toes. Their wings reached almost to the ground. One of the angels had what appeared to be a harp and another had her arms out-stretched towards Christ.'

She said the vision did not appear to be cloud formation. It did not move. The picture appeared gradually and then slowly faded away, lasting in all about two minutes.

Strangely reminiscent of the Angels of Mons in the First World War, the vision appeared at about 11am on the first Sunday in September, by day and by time the anniversary of the outbreak of war.

Five Ashes

The pub here is The Five Ashes (what else) and for more than 60 years it was very much a family concern. The old building was once a farmhouse and the great-grandson of the owner, Alfred Berwick, held the licence with his wife from 1914 until retirement in 1959 when their daughter Rosie took over. She became Mrs Cloke on her marriage and the long family association ended in 1977 when she and her husband retired to Crowborough.

The Eastwood family have been key figures in giving Five Ashes its communal buildings. Boaz Eastwood helped to erect an old army hut from Eastbourne which served as the village church, and his son Roy was a leading light in the fund-raising campaign which built the village hall in 1976.

'Twitts Ghyll' was once the home of Sir Austen Chamberlain, son of the great Joseph, who was Chancellor of the Exchequer in 1903 and Foreign Secretary in the 1920s. He came here to escape the cares of Parliament and expand his collection of rock plants, which came from all over the world. He had green fingers but lazy feet. Only once did anyone in the village see him walk the half-mile to Five Ashes and back.

Fletching 🌿

The children at the village primary school have good reason to remember the Jolly Butcher of Fletching with affection. Leonard Allcorn, who died at the age of 74, stated in his will that £200 of his estate be used to give the local youngsters a bumper party. His wish was duly observed with mountains of cakes and jelly, plus a special musical performance from a theatre company.

Mr Allcorn also left a legacy for sausage lovers. His famous 'herbie' pork variety put the village on the map, with people travelling many miles to stock up, and the recipe was passed on to his successor behind the butcher's counter, Mr Graham Smith.

Fletching Bonfire Society may be one of the smallest in the county but it has a history stretching back more than a century. Every year on a November night the old houses of the compact village street glow in the light of a hundred torches and monstrous shadows are thrown on the walls as the bonfire revellers march in procession to the site of the blaze and firework display. Fletching's members lead the way, dressed in uniforms of the American Civil War, and they are followed by the gaily dressed members of the visiting societies who come along to give their support and make the evening a success.

A tradition that has died used to be observed on May Day when the children had a holiday and went round the village with flower-decked maypoles singing 'Maypole, Maypole, please remember the Maypole' and were given money for their creations. They later trooped across to Sheffield Park where the maypoles were laid on the lawn and judged by Lord Sheffield.

Edwardian childhood days were recalled by Mrs. W. Butcher in a book on the village's past produced by members of the Forget-Me-Not Club. She wrote: 'At Splayne's Green there was an oak tree which we called The Haunted Oak and we used to run like mad past it. I don't know what we were frightened of; some childish thing I expect. I think it was something to do with the devil.' Another source of the delicious thrill of fear was the unfortunate Abednego Weston who lived at the Rose and Crown. This 'funny, nearly square man with hardly any hair' was teased by the youngsters who called him Mr Bednigo, and he would chase after them as best he could, waving a stick.

Simon de Montfort and his army camped here on the eve of the Battle of Lewes in 1264. They are supposed to have spent the night in vigil before making their way through the dawn countryside to victory on the Downs above the county town, and legend says that those knights who were killed were carried back to Fletching and buried in full armour beneath the church.

In the church, which was new when de Montfort was here, is a tomb which tells a sad little love story. It bears the recumbent alabaster figures of Richard Leche (died 1596) and his wife Charitye, though she was still alive when it was made. After his death she married the second Earl of Nottingham who was as unkind to her as her first husband had been kind. So 'shee of her own accorde caused this monument to be made and herself livinge, to be pictured lying by him as you see.'

There is also a small brass to glover Peter Denot (1450), a supporter of Jack Cade's ill-fated rebellion, with a simple inscription and a pair of gloves to indicate his trade.

Arrows were the big business here at one time, supplying both the heads and flights to the ammunition that won the battles of Crecy and Agincourt for England. There is nothing to indicate, though, that the village got its name from the fletchers who applied the arrow feathers.

In later years there were several hop gardens in the parish and the school holidays were timed for hop-picking, the children lending a hand at earning the money which went towards winter clothing. Miss D. Martin remembered that at the turn of the century the month long summer holiday was spent every day at Searles hop garden from 8am until 4.30pm when the head man cried 'Pull no more pales.' At the end of the season the young pickers were rewarded with a tea party at Mr Maryon Wilson's riding school.

A more undercover local pursuit is found in the old Sussex proverb: 'The people of Fletching live by snapping and ketching'. This implies there was a fair amount of poaching went on to supplement rural incomes.

Folkington

There are strong links with nature in 'Fowington', a shy little place where they used to cultivate teasles specifically for the dressing of Broadcloth.

Fifty years ago it was noted for its herd of Sussex cattle and in the 1960s the village played its part in getting a better deal for badgers. Lady Monckton's attention was drawn to setts in the area (where two local youngsters had discovered an unexploded bomb), her interest was kindled and with the help of her cousin Lord Arran she later introduced the Badger Protection Act in the House of Lords. Ironically, in more recent years the village has been the focus of national controversy over the laying of traps to catch the badgers, which are held to be responsible for spreading bovine tuberculosis among cattle.

Nicholas Culpeper, the famous herbalist, lived at Folkington. After being apprenticed to an apothecary he set himself up as a 'student of physic and astrology' in the 1640s and discoursed at length on the healing arts of his era. He is probably best known for his *Herball* reprinted many times.

Inside the 13th century church is a memorial to Viscount Monckton, who had the role of adviser to King Edward III, and to Lady Barbara Thomas, daughter of Sir Herbert Springett (see Ringmer), who died in 1697. 'Goodlyness was her imployment and Heaven is her reward.'

Forest Row

Ashdown Forest was for centuries a royal hunting ground but the parties chasing wild boar and deer needed somewhere to relax after a long day in the saddle. Forest Row was where the hunting lodges were built, and that is the origin of the settlement, though it was not until the railway station was opened in 1866 that there was any substantial development and it did not achieve full parish status until 1894. The Royal Ashdown Golf Club was opened in 1888 and was only the second golf course established in Sussex, the first being at Seaford.

Among the most interesting local buildings is Kidbrooke Park, which was built in 1724 for Lord Abergavenny after a fire at Eridge Park. The house has fine Adam style plaster ceilings and the magnificent surrounding parkland was laid out by Humphrey Repton, one of the most celebrated landscape gardeners of the time.

The house has seen many owners. It was bought in 1921 by Olaf Hambro, chairman of Hambros Bank, and he and his wife took a great interest in the garden. Hambro helped to finance an expedition to the Himalayas by Kingdon-Ward who brought back a blue poppy and a new strain of gentians which were grown for the first time in England at Kidbrooke. The late Queen Mary, wife of King George V, came to Forest Row to see the blue poppy.

Hambro sold the house in 1938 after the death of his wife. In 1945 it became a Rudolf Steiner school, Michael Hall School. The village has become something of a mecca for supporters of the Rudolf Steiner methods of education; it also houses Emerson College.

Another educational establishment in Forest Row, Ashdown House preparatory school, was given a royal seal of approval when it was chosen by Princess Margaret and Lord Snowdon for their son, Viscount Linley, and the couple were regular visitors to the village while he was a pupil there. The house, built in 1795, was designed by Benjamin Latrobe before he emigrated to the USA.

The Brambletye Hotel featured in literature in a story by Sir Arthur Conan Doyle who lived at nearby Crowborough. Sherlock Holmes, the doyen of all detectives, stayed here in the story *Black Peter*. The hotel now has a 'Black Peter's Bar' of course.

Wall Hill was the scene of an infamous robbery in 1801 when the mail coach was held up at pistol point and robbed of about £12,000. Two brothers named Beatson were convicted of the crime and sentenced to death. They were brought from Horsham to the scene of their crime, riding in a cart and sitting on their own coffins. A gallows was erected close to the spot where the robbery took place and the Beatsons were hanged at noon on April 7, 1802, watched by a crowd of about 3,000 people.

Charles Abbot, Speaker of the House of Commons, who was

living at Kidbrooke Park at that time, requested that the bodies be taken down from the gibbet before his wife returned home from London, as he feared the sight would distress her.

Framfield 🦡

The approach to the parish church is one of the loveliest in the county, a row of Tudor houses which form the core of the village, but the old church itself has given the good people of Framfield more than their fair share of headaches over the centuries.

Built in the 13th century, one of the first in Britain to be dedicated to St Thomas a Becket, much of it was destroyed in a disastrous fire in 1509 and the parishioners petitioned Henry VIII to grant his approval for churches in four counties to give financial help towards its repair. Then in 1667 a second calamity occurred: The tower of the church collapsed one Sunday just after the faithful had departed from morning service. The villagers seem to have shrugged off what was almost a major tragedy and made do without a tower for a couple of centuries, when the bells (one of which bears the delightful inscription 'Oblige me not to call in vain') were rehung in the new structure. A rather obstinate churchwarden in Victorian days built himself a chimney and grate in his pew, no doubt for a little creature comfort during the sermons. It apparently took a lot of persuasion from the congregation to get him to remove it.

It was thanks to the reforming zeal of the Reverend Henry Hoare in the 1840s, records Herbert Keef in his description of the church, that the building was saved from utter ruin arising from the scandalous neglect of the responsible Church authorities.

Framfield was the birthplace, in 1834, of Robert Realf, a poet from the age of 15 and a leading campaigner in the fight against slavery. After emigrating to America he did missionary work in the slums of New York. He met the great abolitionist John Brown who proposed to make him Secretary of State in his government. Following Brown's capture at Harper's Ferry, Realf was arrested but later released and he joined the Union Army in the Civil War, writing war songs to cheer the spirits of the Yankee soldiers, and when he left the Army he established a school for

FRAMFIELD CHURCH

freed slaves. He killed himself at Oakland, California, in 1878. A sad end for a man who achieved so much for people so far away from his own roots.

Framfield's older inhabitants might think twice about repeating the courageous action of their forebears. In 1792 it is recorded that a cricket team composed entirely of the village's septuagenarians challenged any village in Sussex to a game. Unfortunately no details exist of any such match taking place; maybe nobody dared risk the ignominy of a thrashing from the old 'uns.

Frant

There are happenings both bizarre and eerie connected with the village churchyard of Frant. Eighteen-year-old John Havey was killed in 1818 when he was hit by a stone falling from the church tower. The fatal lump of masonry was used as the footstone to his grave.

Forty years later, when Sir Henry Thompson was rector, the

church underwent extensive alterations including enlarging the chancel which meant the removal of tombstones belonging to the Budgen family. One of the graves was a young woman who died on her wedding day and was buried in her bridal gown. There was said to be a curse affecting anyone who disturbed her resting place. In extending the chancel her coffin was accidentally broken. Sir Henry and two other present at the time all died within the year...

On the same theme, the yew tree which had stood in the churchyard for more than 250 years was blown down in a violent gale in 1928. Remarkably, no damage was caused to the tombstones in its fall.

From the lofty heights of Shernfold Park you can see Dover. This house was the retirement home of Colonel John By of the Royal Engineers, a Peninsular War veteran who went out to Canada to superintend the construction of canals. In 1826 he founded Bytown which has since developed into Ottowa. The fact that he had spawned one of Canada's great cities was all in the future of course, but it seems a little harsh that at the time Colonel By was much criticised for overspending his canal budget. He retired to Frant to lick his wounds.

He was not the village's only link with Canada. During the Second World War Canadian troops were billeted in the area and made themselves popular with the locals. So much so that when the war was over it was decided to dig oak saplings out of the woods near Bayham Abbey which were shipped across the Atlantic to form part of the Canadian Air Force Memorial.

Stratford Canning, Lord Stratford de Redcliffe, was one of the great diplomats of the 19th century. His most notable achievements were as ambassador in Turkey where his status was almost that of a sovereign at a foreign court. He exercised his influence to effect internal reforms and safeguard the rights of Christians in Turkey. He had become so closely connected with Turkish policy that when he was nominated ambassador to Russia in 1833 the Tsar refused to receive him. Lord Stratford de Redcliffe built Frant Court in 1859 and lived there until his death at the age of 94 in 1880. He was buried in the churchyard.

Nearby is a monument to Captain Hans Busk, originator of the Territorial Army, who was born in 1816. As an undergraduate he impressed on Lord Melbourne the importance of rifle clubs and a volunteer army – which eventually became the Territorials.

The church organ was built at the end of the 19th century by Frenchman August Gern who settled in the village. The magnificence of his unique gift to his adoptive community only came to the attention of latter-day residents when it broke down on Christmas morning in 1966 and the grime was removed to see what had gone wrong. It was restored to its full glory by local fund-raising.

A craftsman of a different kind was the sculptor Frank Rosier, whose wood carvings grace several Sussex churches and are, naturally, a prominent feature of Frant's. The village was lucky to have him, and can thank its setting in the high country near the Kent border. Rosier, a consumptive, came to deputise for the post-master while he was away on holiday. He found the altitude and air so beneficial that instead of staying only a fortnight he stayed for the remaining 20 years of his life. Round the outside of his woodcarver's shop he created an eye-catching frieze showing craftsmen at their work.

This was a great sporting community, though there are many in the conservation-conscious 1980s who would be horrified to know that otters in the local streams were a principal quarry of the huntsmen and that one family kept a pack of terriers for hunting badgers in the 1920s.

It is many years since the last 'Fawn Supper', when the Marquess of Abergavenny gave a fawn each year to be cooked for the employees on his estate as a Christmas feast.

Friston 🦋

When fire destroyed East Dean vicarage in 1665 it was the Selwyns of Friston Place who provided a replacement. They gave what is now known as the Old Parsonage and asked in return that a sermon, in memory of the Selwyn family, be preached annually in Friston church. It remained the vicarage until 1936 and just below it was one of the biggest bee farms in England.

Friston, along with its bigger neighbour, sent frequent petitions for a reduction in taxes because the crops were forever being laid waste by French raiding parties during the 14th century. The hamlet is peaceful enough today, with open hills leading to the sea on one side and miles of dense forest land on the other, though it does hold the distinction of being the last parish in the now defunct Hailsham Rural District to have a German bomb dropped on it.

The sea's uncertain moods are reflected in the stark wooden cross in the churchyard which bears simply the words 'washed ashore.' The distinguished composer Frank Bridge (1879–1941) lies here, too. He was a teacher to Benjamin Britten and deputised for Sir Henry Wood at the 'Proms'.

Crowlink, 'The Hill of Crows' which lies closer still to the coast, was the home of the author E. Nesbit, of The Railway Children fame, and the cellars of Crowlink House reputedly stored 'Genuine Crowlink' – smuggled gin which fetched high prices.

History does not record what misfortunes befell Simon Payn that forced him to leave Crowlink and accept Bayham Abbey's charity. What we do know is that in 1290 the Abbot undertook to receive 'Simon Payn of Friston and his wife Emma for as long as they shall live.' His son Henry, daughters Constance and Godiva and four younger children were also to be cared for and the amount of food they were to be allowed throughout the year was carefully recorded.

Simon's descendants seem to have had better luck, returning to Crowlink where they lived for generations. The name Payn is still to be found in the area.

Glynde ꧁

The Glyndebourne Opera House is just over the parish boundary in Ringmer, but over the years it is the name of Glynde that has become synonymous with opera so let's cheat a little. As a world famous centre for that art, the al fresco champagne picnics on golden summer lawns have become just as much a part of the social calendar as Ascot, Badminton or the Centre Court at Wimbledon.

The opera house, opened in 1934, was created by John Christie who inherited the Tudor house which stands beside it and a fortune from his father on condition that he did something good with his life. Music, and opera in particular, were the great loves of this former Eton science master and so that was his gift to the world in a building designed for him by Edmond Warre. It had a mellow look from the start for Mr Christie spent years collecting weathered bricks to make the opera house blend with its surroundings.

Glynde also produced an art form on four legs in the South Down sheep. John Ellman lived here for 60 years until the dawn of the Victorian era and during that time reformed and refined the thin, scraggy and coarse-woolled sheep of Sussex. He developed a breed that retained its small stature, was a pleasant mixture of fat and lean with the sweetness that comes from hilly pastures. In addition to bringing the dinner tables a superior mutton he brought about a similar improvement in the quantity and quality of the wool.

Ellman's success as a breeder made him a wealthy man and Glynde a place of agricultural pilgrimage. He was a model employer, lodging all his unmarried servants in his own house and when they married giving them a cottage and enough land for a pig, a cow and a garden. He built the school and kept the village free from public houses. At the annual Glynde sale rams often commanded three-figure fees and sheep were transported all over England, and to New Zealand, South Africa and Australia.

Ellman's Home Farm was later the residence of one of the most famous soldiers of the Queen, Field Marshal Viscount Wolseley.

The village huddles under the massive dome of Mount Caburn and the Romans are supposed to have cultivated grapevines in these parts. Perhaps this prompted one cynic of long ago to christen a valley of the hill Vinegar Bottom.

Apart from the great arch in the shape of a horseshoe at the old village forge, Glynde's most striking piece of architecture is its church, a controversial Grecian creation built for Bishop Trevor in 1763 on the site of an old church that was falling down. It has been variously described as being 'in very bad taste' and 'uninteresting, chiefly because it is quite out of the picture'. Others have spoken of its elegance and charm.

Glynde's musical traditions have roots deeper than Glyndebourne and are of a more earthy nature. The Glynde and Beddingham Brass Band was formed in 1925 by the village station master Mr Turner. And at the diamond jubilee celebrations members paid tribute to Bert Beech, who joined the band at its formation. Bert started as a cornettist at the age of nine, but switched to the euphonium when the cornet became too much for his teeth. When the band reformed at the end of the Second World War the euphonium was found to be riddled with machine gun bullets, apparently inflicted by the Home Guard.

William Hay, born at Glyndebourne in 1695, was scarcely five feet in height, had a hump-back and misshapen limbs. But he was elected Member of Parliament for Seaford and became Keeper of the Records at the Tower of London, in addition to travelling widely and writing essays and poems. He wrote an essay on deformity, describing in a pleasant, bantering style how he had come to terms with his afflictions, in which he states: 'When I am in a coach with a fair lady, I am hid by silk and whalebone. When I sit next her at table, my arm is pinioned, I can neither help her nor myself. We are deprived of the pleasure of seeing each other; she would scarce know I was there if she did not sometimes hear me under her wing. I am in Purgatory, on the confines of Paradise! I therefore beg one favour which she may grant with honour, that – since I despair of supplanting her lap-dog – she will allow me a cushion to raise me above such misfortunes.'

Edward Boys Ellman, in *Recollections of a Sussex Parson,* relates how the Misses Tuttee at Glyndebourne once made a complaint to his grandfather 'of boys bathing within sight of their house, in a pond, and that it was a most indecent sight for any lady to see. The boys, on being spoken to on the subject, said they were so far off that they were sure the ladies could not have seen anything indecent, unless they stared at them through a glass.'

Groombridge

The river Medway forms the county boundary and cuts right through Groombridge. A mighty clout from the cricket pitch would be Kent's problem, not Sussex's.

Old Groombridge lies in Kent but East Sussex can lay claim to a heroine in the community which has grown around the railway station. The late Julie Tullis was a member of the expedition which in 1985 made the maiden attempt to climb Mount Everest from the north east ridge. They were beaten back short of the summit by bad weather, but Julie can point to being the first British woman on the world's highest mountain.

Guestling 🦪

The close proximity to the seaside resort of Hastings has in recent years brought demands on the village to play its part in the leisure and tourist industry, with proposals for a new 'village' of holiday chalets and a golf course.

Industry of the more conventional kind flourishes here. Hand-made bricks are made in Fourteen Acre Lane, where the Hastings Brickworks has a claypit. Modern bricks would look out of place in a building of antiquity so there is a great demand for the Guestling variety, produced by specialists. Church restorers are particularly grateful to the business and other customers have included Camber Castle, Hampton Court and Buckingham Palace.

A 'Guestling' was a sort of parliament instituted by the Cinque Ports Confederation to sort out matters among themselves and negotiate with other seaport towns. It probably took its name from the village.

Adam Ashburnham, a member of a family that lived here for 400 years, made a bequest in his will for someone to put in a good word for him after his death: The sum of 4s 4d a year, with meat and drink at the manor house, was left to the priest who would pray for Adam's soul and for the souls of his friends.

The Cheyneys were another important family who wanted to be remembered on earth; the 17th century effigies of John and Elizabeth Cheyney in the church chancel were to be kept clean, and land was left to 'four poor widows' to ensure that this was done.

One of England's great scholars when Shakespeare was born

was Gregory Martin, born in the old timbered house called Maxfield to the north of the village. He became a tutor in the house of the Duke of Norfolk and spent the last years of his life at Rheims, where he translated the Latin Bible into English, a version known as the Douai Bible. He died in 1582 and is buried in Rheims.

Buried in Guestling is that most celebrated of all nannies, Alice – she of the changing of the guards at Buckingham Palace. Recently an additional inscription has been added to the headstone explaining who Olive Brockwell was. The new inscription was paid for by Christopher Milne, the original Christopher Robin (see Hartfield). For the past few years there have been no local relatives to look after the grave so the task was taken on by a Rye bookseller, Tony Reavell.

Hadlow Down 🦚

A strange place to find an unusual business, especially one that got the royal seal of approval. The Keston Foreign Bird Farm, proclaimed in 1927 as 'the only farm of its kind in the world', was appointed aviculturalists to King George V and the Duke of Bedford. The exotic birds of the world flourished in this corner of Sussex and the business with them; as Southern Aviaries it was put on the market as a going concern in 1985.

In the middle of the last century Hadlow Down got its school, presided over by a one-legged schoolmaster indelicately known as Cripple Wood by his pupils. It also got its church. It was here that a farmer called Bridger wanted to have his son christened Beelzebub. The parson refused and Mr Bridger settled for Augustus.

The Spotted Cow and The Stonemason's Arms, together with a little ale house in Tinker's Lane famous for its home brew, have long gone. But The New Inn survives as the village's hostelry. It replaced the old pub on the site which was burned down, some said deliberately, in the 1880s when the bailiffs were about to move in and take away belongings.

Passing through the village on the main road it does not seem to be a place of much antiquity. It is the older houses to the north and south of the village ridge which bear testament to a prosperous community during the days of the Sussex iron industry. Something even earlier is the acre of land near Shepherd's Hill surrounded by a 20ft wide pentagonal moat, now much silted up. It was not the site of a castle or fort; the theory is that it was once a secure place for the women and stock against attacks from wolves when the menfolk were away hunting. Its age is indeterminate, but The Moat was scheduled as an ancient monument in 1968.

Halland

The hospitality at the big house, principal family seat of the Pelham family from 1595 until 1768, was lavish enough to prompt the diarist Thomas Turner (see East Hoathly) to put pen to paper:

'The ale was strong at Halland House, and it flowed as freely there as it did in other old halls, in what are called the days of the 'fine old English gentleman'. Many a bout we had of it. I may safely assert that when we have met in the hall upon any occasion, political or otherwise, not one of us has returned home thoroughly sober.'

The building was dismantled at the end of the 18th century and used as a source of building materials when the Pelhams deserted Halland for Stanmer.

Architecture of our own century caused an outrage here in the 1930s when Serge Chermayeff's design for the house Bentley Wood was found so shocking by the Rural District Council that it refused planning permission. Client and architect won the day at a public inquiry, and the glass and cedar wood home is still striking in the 1980s.

Local legend asserts that Terrible Down was the scene of one of England's 'forgotten' battles, when fugitives from Henry III's beaten army at the Battle of Lewes turned to face their pursuers and were massacred. Another version is that Alfred the Great clashed with an army of marauding Danes. Both tales describe with relish that the slaughter was so great the combatants waded 'ankle deep' in blood and that the streams ran red.

Hamsey

Walk down the narrow lane that ends at the church, perhaps framed at dusk by the neon glow of Lewes to the south, and it's a journey straight out of Charlotte Bronte or Charles Dickens at their atmospheric best, with perhaps a shade of Hammer Horror. This mysterious place with its medieval church, complete with gargoyles, standing on a lonely island in the middle of the Ouse Valley, is hardly big enough to be called a hamlet. But it was not always so isolated and remote. Once it was the ham of the de Say family and it was perhaps a village that died and disappeared by choice.

Near the site of the beautiful old church a fortified manor house once stood and a thousand years ago the Saxon King Athelstan held a meeting of his counsellors at Hamsey, so it must have been a well established centre of some significance. Legend says the village was almost completely wiped out by the plague and that the surviving inhabitants chose to sacrifice themselves by refusing all contact with neighbouring areas for fear of spreading the disease. Food supplies dwindled and the village slowly starved to death. Did it ever happen? The experts say there is no real evidence to suggest that it did, but it is a romantic yarn in keeping with the enigmatic feel of Hamsey.

Certainly Offham, a mile or so away from the flatlands, became the new village and Hamsey church fell into disuse being reduced eventually to the status of a mortuary chapel. It was not until the 1920s that parishioners rallied round and raised the money for a thorough and sensitive restoration. The building is now closed during the winter but takes on a new lease of life in the summer when monthly services are held there by candlelight and coachloads of people descend on Hamsey to savour the special charm of the place.

The church remembers three generations in a century who each lost a John by war. John Bridger Shiffner died fighting under Wellington in 1814, another John Shiffner fell in the Crimea in 1855, John Shiffner, the sixth baronet, was killed at Gricourt in the last year of the Great War.

Hartfield ✥

The rules of Hartfield Workhouse in 1821 were enough to inspire a morbid fear of falling on hard times: 'It is required that every poor person who is supported in this House, either man, woman or child, shall attend Divine Service every Sunday morning and afternoon and on all Prayer Days throughout the year, by order of the Governor or Governess. All those that neglect Morning Service shall have no Dinner. Those that neglect the Afternoon Service shall have no Supper.'

It was also the custom when people first applied for poor relief of sending them out on Ashdown Forest with a wheelbarrow to bring back a load of stones. Presumably this back-breaking task was designed to make people think twice about asking for aid.

This is forest country, and the history of the village is closely linked with earning a living from the acres of heath and woodland which stretch away to the south. Hartfield men managed some notable 'firsts' on Ashdown, one Colonel Young introducing sheep to the forest and a shepherd to look after them in the mid-19th century, and Mr Bernard Hale brought Shetland cattle to the area.

Mr Hale and his labourer John Miles were involved in a long drawn out trial in 1876 which was to decide the future of the area. The seventh Earl De La Warr, Lord of the Manor of Duddleswell and owner of the soil, brought a test case against these two 'Commoners' ordering them to refrain from cutting litter on any part of Ashdown Forest. The Earl lost his case on appeal and a Board of Conservators was born, chosen by the Commoners themselves, to protect traditional rights and privileges. Byelaws were introduced which made it illegal, among other things, to use blasphemous or obscene language on any part of the forest, or to light a fire without authority.

The Board today maintains the forest as laid down in the Ashdown Forest Act, 1974, as a 'quiet and natural area of outstanding beauty.'

Hartfield is a place where grown-ups can indulge in a little nostalgia. This is the territory for the adventures of Winnie-the-Pooh for their author, A.A. Milne, lived in the village.

Posingford Wood and Five Hundred Acre Wood are where many of the escapades took place and the bridge where Pooh and Christopher Robin played 'Poohsticks' has become a place of pilgrimage. The parish council has in recent times had to take steps to repair the footpath leading to the bridge, but it has received some financial help with the work from Methuen, publishers of the Pooh stories.

Three centuries ago Nicholas 'Beggarman' Smith undertook some unusual market research. This wealthy man disguised himself as a beggar and wandered from village to village to find out the nature of Sussex folk. He met with little kindness until he came to Hartfield where he got a warm welcome, put down roots at Crotchford Manor and left £10 to be shared in perpetuity by 40 poor people of the village in his will of October 1634. Remarkably, 'Beggarman' is still honoured every Good Friday morning when there is a short service by his grave.

Inside the graceful 13th century church is a tablet to Richard Randes, a rector of Hartfield who died in 1640, presumably written by himself in Latin which translates in part as: 'He lived obscure and always shunned the vulgar throng, that is wont to reek of the odours of vine crowned Bacchus. But alas! he lived badly and now imprisoned in the darkness of the tomb, he teacheth thee what he late began to learn himself.'

Hellingly

> Herrinly, Chidd'nly and Hoadly,
> Three lies, and all true.

An old rhyme of which most counties seem to have a version, but a look on the map will show that in this case the three parishes at least adjoin each other. Many of Hellingly's residents are unaware that they belong to the parish, however, because the boundary is deep inside the northward expansion of Hailsham.

It can cause headaches for the parish council but clerk Bert Crouch takes it all in his stride, as he has with the intricacies of running Hellingly for nearly half a century. Since the parish council was formed in 1894 there have been only two clerks, which must be something of a record. Mr Crouch succeeded Mr A.C. Richardson in 1939 and 40 years later was presented with a gold-plated pen set by the councillors to mark the occasion. The problems facing the worthy representatives of the parish have not changed all that much since he took his place at the table, said Mr Crouch.

The Rev Frank Fox-Wilson was a rector here in recent years whose artistic talents helped fill the church coffers. His carvings of wildlife were sold at auction and prompted some spirited bidding.

One of his forebears was John Milles, a Protestant rector who died for his faith as one of the 300 victims of Queen Mary, being burned at the stake in Lewes in 1557.

Horselunges, a moated Tudor mansion, was the scene of a bizarre 'miracle' during the reign of Henry VI. Quite how young Agnes Devenish managed to get a plum stone lodged in one of her nostrils is a mystery. But it must have been extremely uncomfortable and later led to fears that Agnes would die. Her mother invoked the 'blessed king' – and the stone fell out.

There was a murder at Horselunges which must have caused a local sensation in 1541 in the days when it formed part of the Pelham family's hunting ground of Laughton Chase. Thomas Fiennes, Lord Dacre of Herstmonceux, planned a little illegal deer hunting with a group of friends one April night but at Pikehay in Hellingly they got involved in a row with three local men which ended in a fight in which one John Busbrig, Sir Nicholas Pelham's gamekeeper, was mortally wounded. Three men with Lord Dacre were executed and the young lord, after being tried by his peers, went to the scaffold as well, the execution going ahead after what must have been an agonising five-hour wait in vain for a pardon from King Henry VIII. It was the first time in English history that a man of noble birth was executed for killing a commoner.

The heart of Hellingly is a charming array of old cottages around the oval shaped churchyard which rises seven feet in some places above the roads around it. It is the only "ciric" or Celtic burial ground in Sussex to be preserved intact. The dead were lain in raised circular mounds because they were dry and because the circle was the old pagan symbol of immortality.

Towards the end of the 1897 an area of 400 ares at Park Farm, Hellingly, was offered by the Earl of Chichester to Sussex County Council for £16,000 as the site for an asylum. Hellingly Hospital, known to old village residents as 'The Top', was opened in 1903 as the East Sussex County Mental Hospital and remained as such until the National Health Service was introduced in 1948. It is now the psychiatric hospital for a large area of East Sussex and Kent and provides accomodation for some 1,400 patients with a further 60 at nearby Amberstone Hospital.

Today the hospital community is accepted as part of village life, but in the early days the stark and enormous red brick structure must have caused a lot of comment. Efforts were being made to humanise it soon after its opening. The Hailsham Historical and Natural History Society has an Edwardian photograph of the hospital soon after its completion bearing the legend: 'Hellingly Asylum', together with the words 'Wishing you a happy Christmas.'

A scheme was mooted in 1792 to construct a canal from the river Ouse near Beddingham to Horsebridge Mill to open up this part of the county for better trading, but the project was abandoned. The mill was seriously damaged by fire in 1908 but was rebuilt and remained busy grinding not only English corn but Rumanian and Canadian as well until its closure by Ranks Ltd in 1969.

Coager cakes are an old Sussex speciality based on pastry left over from pie making. Mrs Pont, a native of Hellingly, kept a tasty link with home when she emigrated to South Africa. Her method was to roll out the pastry in thin rounds about the size of the top of a teacup. In the middle put quite a small knob of butter, a half-teaspoon of moist sugar and about four sultanas. Catch it all up round to the middle, press and put a little bit of pastry on the top and bake in the ordinary way.

Herstmonceux

This is the home of the trug, the oval shaped wooden basket that is a Jack-of-all-Trades in the garden and home. Trug making is a traditional craft that has been established in Sussex for at least

HERSTMONCEUX CASTLE

200 years but was first brought to the attention of a wider audience by Thomas Smith of Herstmonceux, who displayed his wares at the Great Exhibition in 1851. Queen Victoria displayed such an interest that she ordered several trugs in various sizes which were delivered in person at Buckingham Palace by the enterprising Mr Smith, who travelled all the way there and back on foot.

The word trug is derived from the Anglo Saxon 'trog', meaning a wooden vessel or boat shaped article. The industry thrives to this day and they are still primarily hand-made. Work begins with the rim and handle of sweet chestnut which is split with a cleaving axe and smoothed with a draw-knife. All the waste wood is then used to fire a copper, to create steam, which is used to bend the sweet chestnut around wooden formers. The boards that form the base of the trug are made from cricket bat willow, cut thin, and then shaped and shaved smooth. The willow boards are dipped in water to make them pliable and then nailed into the chestnut frame.

The village was also once known for its sweets. But the little factory has, alas, ceased to produce the colourful hard-boiled creations here.

The moated Herstmonceux Castle, which in 1946 became the home of the Royal Greenwich Observatory, is one of the earliest important brick buildings in the country. It was built in 1441 by Sir Roger Fiennes following the fashion that was popular in Flanders, and it is likely that the bricks were made by Flemish workmen specially imported for the job.

Sir Roger's decendant Thomas, Lord Dacre, received Anne of Cleves on her arrival in England in 1540 but who 'being a right towardly gentleman' was executed on Tower Hill at the age of 23, ostensibly for having caused the death of one John Busbrig while poaching with friends at Pikehay (see Hellingly), but more probably because of 'his great estate, which greedy courtiers gaped after, causing them to hasten his destruction.'

Like all castles, Herstmonceux has had its full share of drama down the years: Creepy stories (like the heiress who was starved to death in her room by the governess), double dealing to match 'Dallas' (like the cunning second wife who plotted a scheme by which the estates would pass to her own family), and ghosts (like the nine feet high phantom of Agincourt who walked the battlements beating a drum). But this was held by many to be one of the Dacres, long thought dead, but living in concealment and drumming to keep potential suitors away from his wife. The most likely explanation is that those indefatigable smugglers made the noise to scare people away while they went about their business.

But the story most likely to find a place in today's popular press concerned Georgiana Shipley, beautiful daughter of the Bishop of St Asaph, and Francis Hare-Naylor, handsome but reckless eldest son of the Canon of Winchester and heir to Herstmonceux Place, which had superseded the castle.

The Bishop tried to discourage their relationship and on seeing Francis arrested for debt while out in the family coach completely washed his hands of him. Francis returned disguised as a beggar and in 1785 he eloped with the lovely Georgiana. They lived in Italy and had four children before Francis inherited Herstmoneux Place on the death of his father. Georgiana was as eccentric as she was beautiful. She was often seen riding about the grounds and village on a white ass; insisted on the family conversing in Greek at meal times; and went to church accompanied by her white doe, which rested at the end of her pew.

The castle, which had become ruinous after the building of Herstmonceux Place, was restored in 1929 by Colonel Claude Lowther, who had raised three battalions in the Great War known as Lowther's Lambs, the task being completed in the 1930s by Sir Paul Latham. With the coming of the Observatory, telescope domes like vast mushrooms sprang up in the castle grounds but were not allowed to impair the romantic loneliness of the russet red building.

Herstmonceux is at the heart of a galaxy of tiny satellite hamlets like Flowers Green (where The Welcome Stranger was famous for only selling beer), Stunts Green, Gingers Green, Windmill Hill and Cowbeech. Folk used to pour into the village from the outlying areas on a Saturday night in the days when it had its own cinema.

They are a waggish lot at the Merrie Harriers in Cowbeech and a few years back the regulars thought it their public duty to form the Marsh Mountain Rescue Team (Pevensey Levels, as flat as the proverbial pancake, are only a couple of miles away). The intrepid band were ready for action though, complete with alpine hats, leather shorts, climbing boots and plenty of rope. In the event of fog on their rescue missions a bugle, which made a noise like a pig in torment, was carried to ascertain the whereabouts of the team's leader.

Hooe 🌿

Double weddings can be fraught with problems as two Hooe sisters discovered when they were married to the wrong bridegrooms. The ceremony was conducted in the 1830s by an old vicar who knew the girls but not their young men, and the bridal pairs were wrongly sorted when the service began. Each couple repeated after the vicar in turn the vows, but the men changed names.

Only after the service, when all that remained was the signing of the registers, was the mistake pointed out and the couples asked for a little time to be left alone in the vestry to talk things over. The vicar fretted, having quickly come to the conclusion that the marriages could not be dissolved. He need not have worried; the newlyweds emerged and announced that after due consideration they were quite satisfied with their new partners as they had all known each other for so long. So the brides departed contented, the wives of men whom they had no thought of marrying when they entered the church.

Nathaniel Torriano had been a physician before taking holy orders and becoming vicar here in the mid-18th century. His interest in natural phenomena led to his preaching a sermon after the great Lisbon earthquake in 1756 (felt on the coast four miles from Hooe) which was subsequently printed and widely circulated. A second sermon on the same subject did not have quite the same effect and failed to hold the interest of his people to the extent that Mr Torriano burst out in the middle of it: 'Do not prostitute this house of prayer by turning it into a dormitory!'

The landlord of the Red Lion in the same century was James Blackman, a member of the Groombridge gang of smugglers who took convoys of contraband to Ashdown Forest. Nearby is a cottage haunted by a ghost with singularly regular habits. Every Hallow'een Night it used to be heard as the sound of its footsteps walked across the attic floor dragging a heavy chain.

Horam

Queen Victoria's dung cart and road sweeper has found a new home as part of Neville Cook's rural museum in the village. Over a 10-year period he amassed nearly 4,000 exhibits, from Roman sickles to cheese-making equipment and ploughs.

Victoria's piece of machinery was built in 1898 and used to clean-up the Long Walk at Windsor Castle. It was given by the Duke of Edinburgh to Mr Cook in lieu of cash (at his request) after he had repaired a carriage for the Blues and Royals Regiment. He pledged to keep the royal relic gainfully employed cleaning up the paths at his museum.

Still known as Horeham until fairly recent times, it was the coming of the railway that brought about Horam's expansion. The railway has gone but the village can proudly claim to be a national name thanks to the potent brews of Merrydown, based at the old manor house. From the early beginnings at a cottage called Merrydown in 1946 the wine and cider business has grown to best-seller status and is quoted on the Stock Exchange.

Market gardeners did not have much luck here during the Second World War. The first bomb to fall on Hailsham Rural District blasted Streeton's Nurseries at Vines Cross on July 17, 1940; and the first flying bomb landed on Riversdale Nurseries on June 16, 1944.

Ghosts are not usually associated with the 1980s. Horam provided an exception when a family called for help from the church because their house was haunted by an icy shroud.

Hurst Green ✺

The perils of living at the junction of two busy main roads were captured on camera in an attempt to get a pedestrian crossing here. Unfortunately, the maker of the video film which showed the 'traumatic experience' for old folk of getting across London Road as the traffic flashed by later taped over the evidence with a Noel Coward television special. However, the findings of the film were forwarded to the Department of Transport for consideration.

Traffic apart, this is a vibrant village. It has none of the history of its neighbours but there is plenty going on and the official twinning in 1983 with Ellerhoop, a similar community north of Hamburg in West Germany, has added to the general flavour of activity with both cultural and sporting exchange visits.

Not many small rural communities can boast a clock tower. Hurst Green's was 'erected by public subscription in memory of George Burrow Gregory, of Boarzell, who died March 5, 1892.' It used to incorporate a police house, court and village lock-up but is now used as private offices.

Another village gift that no longer serves the purpose for which it was intended is William Orme Caterson JP's drinking fountain, presented by the master of The Lodge in May 1901. The water supply has been blocked off and the structure seems to have suffered from a collision with one of the cars which cause the community so many headaches.

It is strange to think that there are still people in the village who

MORRIS DANCERS

recall an old gentlemen from an age when warfare had more in common with the Crusades than today's threats of nuclear holocaust. He was Colour Sergeant James Haiter, a Hurst Green man buried at Salehurst in January 1928 at the age of 94. He was the last survivor of the Grenadier Guards who fought in the Crimea.

Icklesham

Helping the needy is an enduring feature here. Today, there is the Five Villages Housing Association with sheltered flats for the elderly on land donated by farmer Dick Merricks in memory of his late son Jim. The association got its name because five villages were involved in raising money for the homes; Icklesham was supported by neighbours Fairlight, Pett, Three Oaks and Guestling.

In the past help came from the likes of widow Elizabeth Cheyney, who in 1710 left half an acre of land and two tenements for the use of two poor and aged unmarried men or women, and from the John Fray bequest of 1592. Unfortunately the money received from this is the same as four centuries ago, a considerable sum then but mere pennies now.

The game of darts is not usually associated with Women's Institutes and even less so with elderly ladies. But Icklesham's WI branch produced a darts queen in Ruby Mann, still a member of the team in her nineties. She switched from archery to darts when the bigger kind of arrows began to prove too much but lost none of her aim for the target. Her secret, said Ruby, was having a good eye for distance and never letting anything stronger than an orange juice get in the way of her concentration.

The village suffers rather through being on the main road from Hastings to Rye, but it can trace its roots back to 772AD and the new town of Winchelsea, ordered by Edward I, was built within Icklesham parish which stretched down to the Rother's mouth. Perhaps this link with the sea gave rise to the church being dedicated to St Nicholas, the patron saint of mariners. Workmen renovating the Norman tower of the building in 1975 uncovered part of the original Saxon church which dated the site back as far as the 10th century.

Another architectural asset is the old smock windmill on Hog's Hill which has found a new role in the last quarter of the 20th century. It is used by Paul McCartney as a recording studio.

One good lady of Icklesham was either much maligned or had plenty of friends in low places. The rolls of the Hundred Court show in 1447: 'That Alice Taillow is a common bawd, and she keeps a suspected house and receives suspected men, whereon the 12 jurors say she is not guilty'. Were the jurors themselves, perhaps, some of the 'suspected men' to return such a unanimous verdict of innocence?

This was one of the few villages recording evacuation plans in the event of the feared invasion of Napoleon; precise livestock records were made in 1798 and everyone given exact instructions on where they were supposed to go. Captain Lamb of the Yeomanry and Provisional Cavalry in Sussex was to be in charge and his instructions included 'Directions for making bread' which involved boiling 2oz of hops for an hour. Hopefully not while the French were storming up the beaches.

In the churchyard are two epitaphs that linger in the mind:

'God takes the good – too good on earth to stay
And leaves the bad – too bad to take away.'

And another on the tombstone of the village schoolmaster, who left a final, lasting message to his pupils:

'Little children, love one another.'

Iden ✿

Cottage industries can usually be relied upon to bring in a modest income, but few have the notable success of Miss Carter of Iden. She started making distinctive jams and preserves at nearby Peasmarsh but moved to her native village in 1929. Queen Mary visited her Still Room in 1935 and even took a turn at stirring one of the coppers of marmalade, which at that time were outside under a lean-to shelter.

The business flourishes to this day, selling to the VIP establishments of Fortnum & Mason and Jackson's of Piccadilly, and exporting all over the world.

This is border country: The flat expanse of Romney Marsh can be seen from here and much of the area is Kentish in character, particularly the fruit orchards which climb the gentle slopes. A breathtaking sight in blossom time.

The county boundary did not deter two sweethearts from staying in touch. The Rev Guy Lockington Bates, son of Iden's rector, would climb to the top of the church tower and signal to his fiancee at Newenden in Kent. After their marriage the couple had twin daughters, to whom proud grandad presented a plot of land adjoining the Parsonage (now Iden Park). The house built on the site is called Twin Sisters.

The village once had its own 'castle', a castellated house surrounded by a moat which was built in 1284 by Edmund de Passeley, with permission from Edward I, and at one time rivalled Bodiam in its magnificence.

In medieval times families often took the name of the place

where they lived and Idens lived here for more than two centuries. Alexander Iden caught and killed the Sussex rebel leader Jack Cade (see Old Heathfield). All that remains of the castle today is a fragment of gateway, standing above the still clearly defined moat. The rest of the building must be under the lanes or incorporated in the cottages.

In a field beside Readers Lane was the site of a herring drying kiln, an indication that the coastline has changed dramatically and that centuries ago herrings came much closer to the village than they do now.

The early years of this century were lively ones for a youngster growing up in Iden, though at one time there were only 29 pupils at the old school, aged from five to 14. Mrs Robbins, born in 1906, recalled the days when you could safely hold a skipping rope over the crossroads beside The Bell in the middle of the village; cooking potatoes under the hop fires in the days when there were three working oasts; collecting acorns for the pigs in autumn; and gathering wool from the hedgerows and fields for pocket money.

The bakery supplied the inhabitants with all the bread they could eat, a blind man with a donkey would collect and distribute newspapers, and a deaf mute and his daughter came round periodically to entertain with a barrel organ.

Mrs Robbins' grandad read books in The Reading Room for the illiterate, and he also distilled elderflower water (a cure for headaches and good for the skin), while his wife was famous for her butter, sold in fancy shapes.

Armistice Day in 1918 was particularly memorable, with all the children playing Land of Hope and Glory on paper-wrapped combs as they danced around a blazing tar barrel.

Iden's 12th century church is mentioned in the Guinness Book of Records as having had only two incumbents in the 117 years from 1807 to 1924, and its belltower is of interest to botanists as it has maidenhair fern, usually only found on West Country cliffs, growing out of the base of the wall on the inside.

Scratchmarks on the windowsill were made by pupils of the old free school, held in a corner of the church, sharpening their slate pencils, but nobody knows the reason why there is a stone fireplace in a second floor chamber of the tower.

One Rogation Sunday a vicar new to the village decided to hold the service in the open air, and as the cricket pitch was the only flat area it was held there just before the Sunday match. Everyone participated, including the cricketers from the visiting team. The summer proved a wet one, and the farmers had such a hard task getting harvest in that one old local moaned to another in the pub: 'That was no good that vicar holding that Rogation service. Look what a job we had with the crops.' His mate looked wisely at him and replied: 'It might not have done the crops no good, but Iden hasn't lost a match this season.'

The smugglers around here – and there were plenty of them – had their own signalling system to evade the revenue men: The hoot of an owl and the cry of a rabbit. You had to be a good countryman to recognise the latter.

Iford

A peaceful farming village, flanked by the Downs and the brooks of the Ouse valley, where the centuries seem to have slipped gently by with nothing to seriously ruffle the pattern of life on the land.

But wartime left its mark, literally, on Iford and gave one little girl a day of excitement she has never forgotten. Now Mrs Dorri Stevens, she was having lunch at granny's cottage in 1942 when a German fighter plane started to open fire on the village. Dorri and grandma scrambled under the kitchen table and when the Messerschmitt had passed over they broke cover and went out to inspect the damage. A bullet had punched a hole through the weathervane of the church and the evidence of that day, though no longer adorning the church spire, is kept inside the building.

Fear of a German invasion brought a proliferation of pillboxes in the river valley, though the menfolk of these parts had their own method of preparing for the enemy. A wartime snap shows them standing proudly beside their handiwork – a machine gun post cunningly disguised as a haystack.

The Ouse once came much closer to the village site and a paved Roman causeway was discovered here some years ago. But the church is Iford's chief glory, built of rough flints like the cottages and walls around it and little changed since it was built in the 12th century. A daughter gave the building a practical memorial to her parents in the form of electric light at a time when far more sophisticated communities were still saying their prayers by oil lamps.

Swanborough is an even smaller place a little to the north which was mentioned in the Domesday Book and boasts a manor house dating in part from the 13th century, once a grange of Lewes Priory three miles away. This hamlet gave its name to a Hundred and a court was held here up until 1860. The late Lady Reading, founder of the Women's Voluntary Service (the 'Royal' came later) lived here and took her place in the House of Lords as Baroness Swanborough.

Isfield 🌿

A small place but a lively one. The Laughing Fish is famous for folk singing throughout the year and every Easter Monday it is the scene of the traditional Tommy Trot Beer Race. The competitors have to carry a half-pint of beer a distance of one mile to the village mill and back within a set time limit, the one spilling the least being adjudged the winner. It is no easy task as the melee surges down the lane and many succumb to temptation after losing a few drops and down the lot.

At The Halfway House there is a noisier contest every year when it stages the Lawnmower Grand Prix. The hopefuls roar round a field behind the pub, with different classes for different types of machine with the cutter blades temporarily put out of action in the interests of toe preservation.

Isfield Station was a victim of Dr Beeching's axe and for many years stood empty and derelict, an eyesore in the heart of the village. Mr Dave Milham stopped the rot in 1983 when he fulfilled a long-standing personal ambition by buying the land from British Rail. He launched himself into far more than just renovation to make a home. He created The Lavender Line, a junior version of the county's more famous Bluebell Line a few miles up the road (see Sheffield Park). The station buildings took on a new lease of life, complete with a proliferation of old fashioned metal advertisement plates, the track was relaid and steam engines returned once more to Isfield. Visitors can now ride a short way up country, but Mr Milham has more grandiose plans in the pipeline.

The station's ghost is still there despite all the changes. It is said to be of a young bride who kissed her husband goodbye for the last time on the platform when he left to fight in the First World War. She committed suicide when news arrived that he had been killed in action.

Isfield's mill is one of the few remaining independent concerns in the county. Water power has long since given way to the more reliable electricity, but the memory of the old days lives on in Clappers Cottage opposite the mill. Clappers was the nickname given to the sluice gates. Perhaps the workmen had to go like the clappers to get them open!

Nearby is a small walled enclosure with a single narrow entrance, believed to be the old pound where stray farm animals were kept and returned to their owners on payment of a fee. The local lads once played a trick on an old carter who had gone indoors to enjoy the hospitality of the mill. In double quick time they dismantled the cart, carried each piece through the pen doorway and then reassembled it on the inside. What the carter said when he returned and found his cart inside the pen and how he got it out again has not been recorded.

In these days of state benefits it is sobering to think that well within living memory the village was the home of Moggy Mothballs. 'Home' for the eccentric Moggy was a cave in the rocks at Buckham Hill, and if the locals had christened her with a less than kind name they were always generous enough to the old lady as she trundled along the lanes pushing an old pram. When Moggy died, a small fortune in notes was found sewn inside the linings of her various coats.

She was given clothes in plenty, but never seemed to get the hang of changing them; one layer went on over another and she resembled a small round ball as she made her perambulations.

The old parish church stands in splendid isolation beside the remains of an even earlier structure, the outline of a Motte and Bailey clearly visible where the old fortification once commanded these upper reaches of the river Ouse. St Margarets once housed the richly sculpted marble coffin lid of William the Conqueror's daughter Gundrada, wife of William de Warenne, founder of Lewes Priory. It was brought to Isfield from the priory at the Dissolution, discovered beneath the floor of the Shurley chapel in 1775 and then returned to the county town.

Across the meadows from the church rises the magnificent Tudor mass of Isfield Place, once the home of the Shurleys. An underground passage is said to link the two buildings and if so it may well have played a part in the local smuggling business which took full advantage of the fact that the river was navigable.

Jevington

Smuggling was once a booming business in this idyllic Downland village, with most of the inhabitants, including the vicars, taking part. The valleys, hollows and high beacons were ideal for those involved in bringing in the contraband from the stretch of coastline between Birling Gap and Cuckmere Haven, and Jevington itself seems to have once had a veritable warren of secret passages and hiding places.

Several lead from the pub, The Eight Bells, where Jevington Jigg, cornerstone of the smuggling operations, was the keeper. Also known as Jack Jigg, James or John Pettit, Wilson, Morgan, Gibbs and Williams to name but a few, he was the crony of Brook (the horse thief), Howell (the tailor,), Rook (the highwayman) and Cream Pot Tom (who met his end at the gallows).

The nocturnal activities of Jevington Jigg soon brought him to the notice of the authorities and in 1788 a body of armed constables 'went to the inn for the purpose of arresting a fellow belonging thereto, whose notorious profligacy and desperate deportment made every precaution necessary to ensure success in attempting to secure his person'. Jigg was playing cards with his friends and on hearing that the inn was surrounded quickly donned a bonnet, cloak, petticoat and spurred boots. He burst outside pretending to have hysterics and made good his escape.

His chequered career kept him in trouble with the law for years but at one point he seems to have been a poacher turned gamekeeper, working for a while with the excise men as a noncommissioned guardian of the revenues. Jigg's pals obviously thought he was an informer and he narrowly evaded a lynch mob.

He could never entirely forget his old habits. He got away with charges of assault and hay stealing and returned to his old haunts after serving part of a seven-year transportation sentence for stealing two hams from one Smith of Jevington. Finally in the summer of 1799 he was convicted of horse stealing at Salisbury and condemned to death. The sentence was transmuted to 14 years at Botany Bay and there, in all probability, he died.

From the time of William Carr in 1670 until the 19th century it seems the 'smuggling parsons' co-operated with what was going on, no doubt to their advantage, and the rectory cellars were so enormous that they could not have been built for anything except the storage of smuggled goods. Among the clergymen who turned a blind eye or actively participated in the illicit goings on was Nat Collier whose curious monument in the church of St Andrew says he died on March 1, 169½. Simon Manningham, Vicar of Jevington from 1734 to 1767, appears to have spoken out against the smuggling racket, a breaking of tradition which caused the clergyman and his flock to drift apart. Manningham wrote the following warning for the man who would take his place:

'August 1754. Look out sharp O my successor, for your parishioners will cheat you wherever they can, neither provoke 'em to anger nor invite 'em to be intimate. My successor if he will not suffer himself to be cheated (as I, poor I, have done) will make of this living above an hundred and fifty pounds a year – S. Manningham.'

The memory of the village's past lingered on into the 20th century, when a handbook to the district published in 1901 noted that a game called 'smuggling' was still popular with local children.

One hapless rector had other things on his mind when the church was presented with a mechanical organ which only played one tune, *Old Hundredth* to which the congregation sang all their psalms. One particular Sunday, after completing *Old*

Hundredth, the organ suddenly went into a lively air called *Little Drops of Brandy.* Frantic efforts to stop it were unsuccessful and the story goes that the rector ran down the lane with the organ still playing in his arms and threw it down the village well.

The same well has a more eerie tale, with the ghostly wails of children said to come from it, and somewhere in Jevington is the Butcher's Hole where the butcher buried his wife after murdering her.

The thorough restoration at the church in 1873 upset the lovers of architecture, with nothing left to be viewed in complete originality in a building dating from Saxon times, and the church bells were carted away to London to be sold. This spawned the jingle:

> 'Jevington folk are very proud people,
> They sold their bells to mend the steeple,
> And before they are left in the lurch,
> They would sell the steeple to mend the church.'

The village once had a monastery in the fields west of the church, but all remains of the building have long since vanished. A court case provides concrete evidence that it was still in existence in 1344. The Prior of Michelham brought action against Adam Elyot, Robert Tut, Thomas Chesham and Robert Qurk for breaking into the Prior's building at Jevington by force of arms, viz: 'Swords, bows, arrows and axes and taking away timber to the value of £20 and committing other enormities against the said Prior.' The defendants denied the charge of breaking in, saying the doors had been open, and put the value of the timber at 12d. The verdict, unfortunately, has not been recorded for posterity.

Kingston ❧

Generations of Kingston boys (and girls) have scared themselves silly by trying to conjure up the ghost of Nan Kemp. Exactly when she lived has got a bit lost in local folklore, but her grisly crime has been handed down (and no doubt elaborated upon) with squeamish relish. Mrs Kemp was said to have murdered her baby and served up the unfortunate infant in a pie for her husband when he came in from the fields. She was in due course hanged and supposedly buried in Kingston's Ashcombe Lane. Local legend said if you ran around her grave three times with your eyes shut her spirit would appear. The exact location of her last resting place also became a little hazy as the years went by, but at the top of Ashcombe Lane is Nan Kemp's Cottage and the grave was always held to be nearby.

The village is in the classic style of the East Sussex Downland community, a single lane of flint cottages and finer houses leading to the foot of the hills. In the middle is St Pancras church, unusual in that it has a tapsell gate at the entrance. The gate swings open on a central axis and is peculiar to the county, others to be found at East Dean, Friston, Jevington and Pyecombe. Wellgreen Lane and The Ridge continued the growth of Kingston but it was the building of a big new housing estate in the 1960s that caused some protest from the established locals. Happily, the village was able to absorb the sudden jump in its population and the estate became the new centre for sporting activities. The opening of the cricket pitch there was a grand occasion as the Kingston worthies took on a Sussex XI. The honour of bowling the first ball went to Tom Tuppen, one of the oldest residents who was playing his cricket for Kingston at a different site long before the Great War took away many of his team-mates.

Tom rather surprised batsman Jim Parks, father of the renowned Sussex and England wicket-keeper of the same name, with an old-fashioned underarm delivery. The old player was taken off complaining loudly that the new pitch was not as good as the old one.

Juggs Lane was the route taken by the Brighton fishwives on their way over the hills to sell their wares in Lewes. The name lives on at the pub, The Juggs Arms, which has a comely version of these stoic ladies as its sign.

Newmarket Hill at Kingston was the lonely Downland eyrie of one of the county's remarkable personalities: John Dudeney, the shepherd scholar. He came to the village at the end of the 18th century as a young man to tend the sheep for a wage of £6 a year, and though he had no regular schooling his thirst for knowledge prompted him to invest what savings he had on books. Some measure of the progress he made can be gauged by the fact that he taught himself to read the Bible in the original Hebrew.

He also studied the ships out in the Channel and built himself a primitive telescope from pasteboard and old lenses to study the heavens. Next, with a pair of compasses and the paper spread on the close-cropped turf, he mastered geometry and simple mathematics. He found it impossible to carry his books and implements with him so dug a large hole, roofed with a stone, to store them on the hill.

Sixteen years later Dudeney descended from the Downs a self-taught scholar to fill the post of schoolmaster. For nearly 50 years he taught science and languages to the youth of Lewes, in addition to the normal curriculum, in an age when elementary schools were a rarity for the poor. His career reached a peak when he played a leading part in the foundation of the Lewes Mechanics Institute.

Laughton ✖

For years, until the arrival of mains drainage, residents had to endure the unkind newspaper catchphrase and headline 'the smelliest village in Sussex.' An unfortunate and unfitting label for a place that was the seat of one of the county's most noble families, the Pelhams.

They lived at Laughton Place, a lonely mansion built by Sir William Pelham ('prudent in peace and valiant in war') during the reign of Henry VIII on the bleak levels below the village. All that remains of the building today is the central tower, though happily this has recently been restored and modernised. It bears the Pelham buckle, crest of the family since Sir John Pelham captured King John of France at Poitiers and was given the buckle of the King's surrendered sword as a keepsake.

Legend has it that a secret tunnel ran from the mansion to the crypt of the village church a good mile away where the coffins of more than 30 Pelhams are interred.

Laughton Place was one of the first brick-built buildings in the county, and the manufacture of bricks was a major industry here; the village once had four brickworks and they were used in the repair of Hastings Castle. The last kilns did not go out until just before the Second World War. Pottery, too, thrived here and continues to do so to this day.

The latter years of the war were tragic for Laughton. A flying bomb landed at Shortgate, killing four people and flattening the main post office and Bell Inn (now rebuilt as The Bluebell).

When the Rev Pearson produced a history of the parish in the 1920s he looked to the Pelham crest for a title, 'The Village of the Buckle'. It is a nickname that has stuck in a community where the population has remained constant since the distant days when folk started to keep count.

The old landlord at The Roebuck used to claim that he was the only mine host in the country entitled to charge for a glass of water. A bit of a stretcher, perhaps, but there was a deal of truth in it. Mains water did not come here until the 1950s and when their wells ran dry in times of drought the locals went to The Roebuck which had a well that never failed and they were able to get their water there. For those that could not get about a water cart would deliver to the door, at a cost. The conditions were so notoriously primitive that no evacuees were sent here during the war.

A ploughman struck lucky in recent years when he unearthed the 'Laughton treasure', a jar crammed with 600 silver halfcrowns bearing the head of Charles I. How this Civil War hoard came to be buried at Park Farm is a mystery, but it is now in a safe place at The Barbican Museum in Lewes.

A belt of Sussex Marble, or Winklestone, stretches under the earth across the Weald in a line from Benenden in Kent to deep inside West Sussex and one of its richest veins occurs at Laughton. Local sculptor Glen Moore has taken advantage of the rich source literally on his doorstep by producing jewellery and other items from this lovely stone, which varies in colour from cream to dark purple.

Litlington ✺

Taking tea, that most British of traditions, was given a new twist at the turn of the century by Mr Russell who added outdoor charm to the affair by introducing the county's first tea gardens. They are an increasing rarity these days, but Litlington's trail-blazer is still going strong.

The clientele can stop off there after taking in this village on the east bank of the Cuckmere with the county's own white horse chalk carving looking down on it all from the hills, not as impressive, perhaps, as those to be found elsewhere, and not as old but still a striking feature.

Mrs Maria Fitzherbert, by tradition, lived at Clapham House before she married King George IV. He seems to have been an energetic suitor, riding 18 miles over the hills to see her.

Little Horsted

Little is the operative word for this village. But despite its humble size it can claim some highly distinguished connections. The Royal Family were friends of Lord and Lady Rupert Nevill who lived at Horsted Place and the congregation at the village church often included the Queen when she paid visits to this corner of the county.

A slightly more tenuous royal link can be found in the grounds of the big house where there flourishes a myrtle bush grown from a sprig out of Queen Victoria's wedding bouquet.

The future of the impressive Victorian mansion as a sort of up-market holiday home became a strong possibility after it was sold by the widowed Lady Nevill to a consortium of Canadian businessmen. But their plans to convert it into time-share flats fell on stony ground.

Lullington

You can count the number of houses on one hand, but the Downland hamlet did claim spurious fame as having the smallest church in England, being only about 16 feet square. In reality, the church of today is no more than the chancel of a much larger building.

A diminutive clergyman with a sense of humour once

preached here, choosing the words 'Jesus wept' as his theme. There were 12 people in the congregation and the collection produced 1/6. The little curate remarked that it was the smallest church, the smallest congregation, the smallest parson, the shortest text and the smallest collection he had ever heard of.

Maresfield ✺

It was quite an occasion when the Duke of Wellington came to stay with Lord and Lady Shelley, who lived at a house called The Cross. At a point on Ashdown Forest his carriage was joined by an escort of 40 mounted farmers and the roadsides were thronged with villagers hoping to catch a glimpse of the Iron Duke, conqueror of Napoleon. Finally the enthusiasts removed his carriage horses and pulled the carriage themselves to tremendous cheering.

The Duke proved a delightful guest, Lady Shelley recorded, but not even she could describe him as a good shot. Taken shooting the next day by his host, he injured a dog, peppered a keeper's gaiters and the arms of an old woman at a cottage window. The gold piece he gave her quelled her shrieks, and she was told to take pride in the fact that she had been shot by the Duke of Wellington.

Many a newcomer to Britain has got his first impression of the country at Maresfield. This used to be a military base and when the troops moved out of the straggling maze of huts it was used as a prisoner of war camp. In later years it housed for temporary periods large numbers of displaced unfortunates: Ugandan Asians and Vietnamese Boat People. The site has gradually acquired a smarter image, with the building in recent years of indoor bowls and sports centres.

Footballer Dixie Dean, Everton's prolific goal scorer, was stationed at Maresfield Camp as a soldier during the Second World War. There are still those who recall with awe his performances when matches were arranged between the camp and the locals.

Though the village is small, the parish is enormous and takes in much of Ashdown Forest, 'The most villainously ugly spot I ever saw,' as William Cobbett, of *Rural Rides* fame described it. The Victorian poet Thomas Pentecost was no more complimentary, describing the forest as

'A heathy waste of huts and dens,
where human nature seldom mends.'

It is doubtful if the thousands of visitors who use the forest each year would agree with these sentiments.

Maresfield once had three ironworks. The last of these was converted into a powder mill in the 19th century. It too has gone, but its ponds remain.

Mayfield ❧

The Devil, a witch and a saint have all played their parts in a colourful past. St Dunstan, who built Mayfield's first wooden church in 960AD, seems to have been a versatile Sussex saint, becoming Archbishop of Canterbury and also finding time to be a skilled statesman, reformer, musician and metal worker.

He had constant trouble with Old Nick and it was while working at his anvil in Mayfield that the Devil came to tempt him in the guise of a beautiful young woman. Dunstan noticed hooves sticking out from beneath the dress and grabbing his red hot pincers from the forge fire seized the nose of the Devil with them. He, understandably, let out a blood-curdling screech and resumed his proper form. In a cloud of smoke he flew away to cool his nose, first in a village spring and then in one at Tunbridge Wells, giving both a sulphurous taste and chalybeate qualities.

The Prince of Darkness was not through with Dunstan, however. According to another legend, he returned in the form of a weary traveller who needed a horseshoe. The saint saw through the disguise again and beat the Devil until he begged for mercy and swore never to enter a house with a horseshoe above the door.

Dunstan is also credited with founding the Palace of the Archbishop of Canterbury beside the church, where the succes-

sors of the saint lived at intervals. When it ceased to be an ecclesiastical residence it was sold off and in 1567 Sir Thomas Gresham, founder of the Royal Exchange, bought the property and entertained Elizabeth I there. In 1864 it was purchased by the Dowager Duchess of Leeds who presented it to the Sisters of the Holy Child Jesus. It was converted into a Roman Catholic boarding school for girls, a purpose it still serves today.

Mayfield's Norman church was destroyed by fire (along with much of the rest of the village) in 1389 and the replacement continued to be a chilly place on a wintry Sunday until two large coke stoves were installed in 1882. One old gentleman was said to have felt the cold so acutely when he took his hat off that a local barrister took pity on him and gave him his old wig, which the rustic sometimes wore sideways by mistake.

The Victorian era saw the end of the feudal custom of ringing the curfew bell each evening at 8 o'clock from Michaelmas to Lady Day (September 29 to March 25). The bell was rung by the sexton who was paid by the churchwardens out of the church rates. There were no funds available to pay the sexton after the Church Rate Abolition Bill was passed, and though voluntary contributions towards his salary kept the bell ringing for a while these soon dried up and a tradition unbroken since Norman times ceased.

Four Protestant martyrs were burnt to death in the churchyard here on September 24, 1556, during the Mary Tudor persecutions. Two of their names were recorded, John Hart, a shoemaker, and Thomas Ravendale, a carrier.

Mayfield must have something of a record in that every vicar from 1780 to 1912 was a member of the Kirby family. There were four of them, starting with the Rev John Kirby (whose fatal flaw was a love of public houses and whose parishioners petitioned for his removal). He was replaced in 1810 by his son, another John, incumbent when the local labourers rioted in the 1830s in protest against their poverty; and the third Rev Kirby was Henry, launcher of the parish magazine, keen ornithologist and a man of considerable courage. In the 1870s he personally nursed back to health a tramp found in a barn suffering from smallpox. Henry was vicar for 52 years, being succeeded at his death in 1897 by his son John, a prominent figure in church affairs who with his wife donated the old village hall.

In 1950 there was a spectacular pageant in the village to mark the bicentenary of the founding of the school. Its first headmaster was Walter Gale, a hard drinker whose favourite tipple was gin by the quartern and whose friends gave him Christmas gifts like a book entitled *A Caution to Swearers.* He supplemented his original wage of £16 per annum by such diverse activities as painting pub signs and carving tombstones, and kept a diary whose pages were in later years saved from being used as firelighters.

'July 2d, 1750 – I went with Master Freeman to Wadhurst; we went to the Queens Head, where we had a quartern of brandy. I went to the supervisor's house, and returned to the Queen's Head, and had three pints of fivepenny between myself and three others; we set out together at 8 o'clock, and being invited to a mugg of mild beer, we went in to Mr Walters'. We left him with a design to cross the fields through Mepham Gill; but it being extremely dark, we kept not long the right path, but got into the road, which, though bad, we were obliged to keep, and not being able to see the footmarks, I had the mischance of slipping from a high bank, but received no hurt. Old Kent came to the knowledge of the above journey, and told it to the Rev Mr Downall, in a false manner, much to my disadvantage; he said that I got drunk, and that that was the occasion of my falling, and that, not being contented with what I had had, I went into the town that night for more.'

Queen Victoria came here as a girl, leaving her silver-topped riding crop as a memento, and the sculptor who engraved the portrait of Victoria which was used on coins in the latter part of her life was Sir Thomas Brook, who is buried in Mayfield churchyard.

The village sign is superb to look at (it won second prize of £500 in a national newspaper competition in 1920) but probably inaccurate. It depicts a young woman and children in a flower covered meadow and indicates that the original name of the village was Maid's Field, though the Saxons knew it as Maegthe (chamomile) and it was Maghefeld in 1295.

The village has remained unpretentious despite its picturesque qualities. The Victorian writer Coventry Patmore describes it as 'the sweetest village in Sussex.' The Timbered Middle House, now a hotel and restaurant, is a real eye-catcher with a tale to tell of matrimonial imprisonment. A landlord of the past had a secret room there where he kept his wife locked away for four years, bringing food up to her on a tray. One version says she died there and that the room is haunted by her thin cries; but the more popular version states she eventually discovered the hidden latch, cracked hubby smartly on the head with the tray when he brought in lunch and made her escape.

By the lights of her time, Alice Casselowe must have considered herself lucky to have got off so lightly when she was accused of being a witch. The records of 1577 state: 'At the Assizes at Horsham Alice Casselowe of Mayfilde, spinster, on the 6th June 1577 at Mayfilde bewitched to death one ox valued at £4 of the goods and chattels of Magin Fowle, gentleman.'

'Another indictment: also on the 1st of June at Mayfilde bewitched to death two pigs at 10s the goods and chattels of Richard Roose. Sentence, one year.'

Fred Wicker was one of the great village characters of more recent years. This blacksmith and sweep also used to help carry the coffins at funerals, rushing in at his rear entrance to remove the soot and coming out at the front suitably attired in black, wearing a top hat or bowler according to the status of the deceased. Then there were the brothers Percy and Jim Skinner, who ran a fish and poultry shop. Knowing that for old ladies with pet cats money was short, Percy would always make sure there was a little extra fish wrapped up in the parcel.

Mayfield's Bonfire Boys and Belles are one of the oldest bonfire organisations in the county. Half the money raised at their autumn celebration goes towards providing a Christmas party for local old folk.

The unusual post mill on Argos Hill was recently restored and has been a feature of the area since 1834, but narrowly escaped demolition during the First World War when it was considered too good a landmark for German Zeppelins!

Mountfield 🪷

They came searching for coal a century ago and instead found gypsum, a sulphate of calcium used in the manufacture of cement and plaster.

The mines of the British Gypsum Company are a series of catacombs which spread over a wide area under the earth. The entrance, too, is hidden away in the woods. The only really tangible evidence of the industry is the aerial ropeway which links the Mountfield mine with another smaller one nearly four miles away at Brightling, the mechanism whispering and creaking as the containers slide stealthily but relentlessly to and fro across the countryside.

Look at a map and join up all the churches, ancient sites and historic buildings and the chances are that you will have roughly a straight line. That is the theory, anyway, behind ley lines which are believed by many to have a pre-Christian significance and sites where lines cross have a special power.

If that is so, Mountfield must be a truly potent place. The Rev Harold Spriggs, vicar here for a quarter of a century, maintained that no less than five ley lines cross at Mountfield church.

The 'X' certainly marked the spot for William Butchers on January 12, 1863, when his plough became entangled with what he thought was a long piece of brass at the Barn Field on Taylor's Farm. He then noticed that it protruded from a square shaped hole in the ground from which he collected a number of other brass objects. They seemed to be ornaments of some kind but the farmer did not display any interest when Butchers showed them to him and said the ploughman could keep them. He made several attempts to sell the strange ornaments and eventually disposed of them for 5/6 – sixpence a pound on a collection weighing 11lbs. It was only later that it was discovered the 'brass' was solid gold, the buried treasure of some Bronze Age chieftain. The Mountfield Hoard, beyond price to archaeologists, eventually fell into the hands of a firm of Cheapside refiners who bought the lot for £550 and then melted it down.

Another Mountfield treasure was treated more kindly. Redecoration in the church in recent years revealed murals dating from the 12th century on the east wall which were badly in need of restoration. Villagers responded in fine style with a series of money-spinning events to boost the special fund set up by the Parochial Church Council.

Netherfield 🌿

The church and the school were designed by the eccentric Victorian architect S.S. Teulon, and built in the middle of the last century by Lady Mary Webster in memory of her late husband Sir Godfrey.

She was a woman of high principle who obviously thought a lot of the village and its people for she kept a secret while the building was in progress. Only when the work was completed did she call in person on the rector and tell him: 'I did not write to you in case you might think I was withdrawing from the project but now that the church is finished and all the bills are paid I must tell you that I have become a Roman Catholic.'

The church is dedicated to St John the Baptist and contains a rather grisly reminder of that fact; a painting of the saint's head on a platter. The artist was Giovanni Barbieri (1591-1666) and it hangs on the north wall.

Newick 🌿

Men of the cloth often have hidden talents but they do not come much more unusual than the late Rev John Baker's. The rector of Newick is a magician – and a semi-professional one at that.

He gave his first public show in 1963 and his repertoire of tricks is now enormous with more than 400 effects and illusions, though he draws the line at fire-eating. 'Presto John', a member of the British Ring and the International Brotherhood of Magicians, regularly baffles audiences with his shows at clubs, schools and playgroups.

Most of his flock have interests outside their normal jobs and careers, too. There are more than 40 different clubs and societies to choose from in a village that has successfully absorbed a massive population boom, rising from 950 to 2,500 since the Second World War.

Those that choose amateur dramatics or cricket are following in some distinguished footsteps: Derek Bogaerde, better-known to the world's cinema-goers as Dirk Bogarde, had his first major stage part with the Newick Amateur Dramatic Society in the 1934 production of *Journey's End* (he is now President of the NADS) and on the cricket pitch the village spawned James and John Langridge in the 1920s.

In a county famous for its cricketing brothers, both played for Sussex and James for England. James was the bowler of the two, while his brother was a batsman and clever slip fielder – a formidable combination and the entry 'caught Langridge (John) bowled Langridge (James)' occurs 133 times in score books.

Among those who encouraged the Langridge boys to develop their skills to the full was Thomas Baden Powell, cousin of the founder of the Scout movement. This small but dynamic eccentric owned much property in Newick and his passion for sport, and cricket in particular, helped him to overcome curvature of the spine and a club foot to be a good all-rounder himself.

Thomas gave the village schoolboys the use of his beautiful private cricket ground where he staged regular matches with his own elevens taking on some high-powered opposition. It was considered a great honour to be invited to play and anyone who refused was never asked again. He staged lavish sportsmen's suppers every year at The Bull, with plenty of free tobacco and drink, and visiting teams always remembered the tea they were provided with at Mr Helmsley's bakery.

Even in his declining years when he was pushed around the village in a wheelbarrow padded in red velvet (a bathchair had proved too uncomfortable) cricket was never far from Thomas' thoughts and when a hairdresser called to give him a trim he found him in bed wearing his cricket cap.

A cricket match at Newick in May 1737 brought one of the most bizarre entries in the Chailey parish registers: 'John Boots killed by running against another man on crossing wicket'. And it was a love of the game that gave the village one of its more peculiar houses. One of Lord Sheffield's butlers used to love watching the cricket on his master's ground (see Sheffield Park) and even after getting the sack was anxious to see the play so he built himself a three-storey house at the highest point in Newick in Allington Road with an additional tower on top which housed a telescope so the butler could get a good view of the cricket three miles away and of the ships in the distant Channel. The tower was later struck by lightning and had to be dismantled.

Memories of Newick in the early years of this century paint a picture of self-sufficiency. It had a snob's (or shoemender); a blacksmith; a shop selling tea, sugar, sweets and shag by the pennyworth; two grocers who also stocked secondhand furniture, lino and carpets; a hairdressers; a tailor (appropriately run by Mr Cutting) and a cottage hospital opened in 1869 to accommodate seven of 'the poor when suffering from non-infectious disease or accident'.

A cattle market was held on the green and a white horse drawn bus plied back and forth from the village to the railway station at 6d a ride.

Queen Victoria's Diamond Jubilee celebrations in 1897 were a day of great festivity and left the village with a useful reminder of the occasion in the form of a parish pump, erected by local plumber Richard Fuller over a well sunk by Arthur and Jack Wood. Church bells rang, a band played and there were sports and tea for the entire village. In the evening there was beer for the men (a limit of two pints each was agreed upon after much discussion), a bonfire and fireworks. The day closed with the National Anthem at 10.30pm.

Elias Hurion Neve was for nearly 50 years master of Newick Boys School in the last century, by all accounts an awesome personality who was assisted in the teaching by his niece Mary Collins, whose addiction to snuff and 'row of flat curls on her forehead' make her sound a formidable character, too. A series of masters were appointed after Elias' death in 1873, none of whom stayed for long. Mr T. Jones was on such bad terms with the school managers that when he resigned in 1881 he recorded in the school log: 'Gave up charge of this school, I trust that my successor will find a smoother way prepared for him than what I had prepared for me, and I hope that by me getting the school in good working order he will merit all the praise; but not from the managers will he get it.'

The girls went to Lady Vernon's School, established by Louisa Barbara Mansell of Newick Place, 'endowed with many virtues and with many accomplishments for amusements and society', who in 1771 gave three cottages as a school and set up a charity to provide a yearly salary for a schoolmistress to teach 12 poor girls from the parish 'reading, writing, needlework and whatever the owner of Newick Park should wish to make them useful servants.' Each girl was allowed 25s a year from the income of the Trust to be spent on clothing and a further £10 made available for the schoolmistress to have an assistant.

Though her school has been absorbed by state education, the Lady Vernon Trust survives to this day and Newick girls are able to draw grants for a wide variety of educational activities.

The old turnpike toll house still stands beside the busy A272 and Blind Lane may well have got its name from the toll fee dodgers, who used it as a bypass well out of sight of the toll house to avoid payments which could be hefty: 'For every horse or other beast drawing a coach 6d; for 1st horse or other beast drawing a wagon 7½d and for every other beast 5d. For a dog or goat drawing any carriage 1d. Drove of oxen cows or cattle 10d per score; sheep, calves or swine 5d per score. For every vehicle moved by steam, gas or mechanism 5s.' Tolls were doubled in the winter months for all laden vehicles.

Ninfield 🦋

Older people in the village still remember Paraffin Annie, also known as Oily Annie. She used to wheel an old pram around the lanes delivering fuel from door to door.

Annie, real name Alice Terry, lived in Manchester Road, Ninfield. An unlikely street name for a place hardly bigger than a hamlet, but there was a good reason. Manchester House, now the village shop and post office, used to be a depot for the Lancashire cotton goods from Manchester, from where they were distributed all along the south coast. The building also had strong smuggling connections and a secret passage is said to link it with Standard Hill House, a quarter of a mile away.

Standard Hill was by tradition the place where William the

Conqueror raised his standard before the Battle of Senlac, a spurious legend which persists in the village sign depicting a Norman knight on horseback. The old house on the site, the home of bird illustrator Basil Ede, is intriguing, with three texts on the outer walls and the date 1659: 'God's Providence is my Inheritance'; 'Except the Lord Build the house they'd labour in vain that build it'; and 'Here we have no abidance.' They seem to have a strong Puritanical theme. Could the latter text simply be a comment on man's brief mortal span or is it a statement to the world at large that no Royalists were hidden away there? If so, this beautiful lettering was almost too late; the Restoration of the Monarchy came in 1660.

One of the treasures in a village that once boasted two windmills is the village stocks and whipping post, beautifully preserved because they are made of iron instead of wood. The transgressors of the law could be catered for in pairs: There are four holes for ankles and four wrist clamps on the upright post. It was here, in 1790, that a wife was sold for half a pint of gin.

The United Friends did its bit for European harmony when Britain joined the Common Market by changing the pub sign to the hands of peace symbol as on the 50p piece.

Northiam ✺

'O rare Norgem! thou dost far exceed
Beckly, Peasemarsh, Udimore and Brede.'

A proud little jingle from the old days. The neighbouring villages probably resented the put down, but certainly Northiam has everything expected of a village: rich in old houses and history, with even a parish pump still there on the green.

The village's water supply was always a headache. Farthings, a late 16th century home reputed to be the first house in the village to have a bath, was where the locals were allowed to take a bucket of water from the pond next to the house by the owner, on payment of a farthing. The name Farthing Pond appears on some of the early maps.

A survey in 1876 revealed that 69 dwellings relied on wells for

their water, 44 on pumps, nine on spring water and six on ponds. Twenty years later it was reported that several houses were without any water supply at all. Some had to bring their drinking water from Stawberry Hole while water for washing was fetched in 'bodges' from the pond at Higham at a rate of 6d a bodge. In 1932 piped water arrived in Northiam but it was not until 1958 that it was supplied throughout the village.

Bark stripping was an important industry in the past, the bark being stripped from oak trees and then taken to the tannery at Tenterden. There were tanyards here, too, and in 1562 one John Robinson along with two others was charged with selling tanned hides in his own house which was illegal.

Excavations in the 1930s confirmed the presence of a glass furnace in Glasshouse Field and further probing unearthed the shed floor and small fragments of pale green window and vessel glass typical of the 16th century. Hops, in addition to the more conventional crops, were a source of income but the most profitable one was, of course, smuggling. There were hiding places like 'the smallest house in Sussex', a one-up, one-down cottage (a family of five once lived there) and secret passages. It was maintained you could get from Newenden in Kent to Northiam and Rye without using a single road!

Not even the Frewen family vaults at the church were sacred when it came to storing contraband and it was also established that children were daring each other to run down among the coffins. The entrance was bricked up to put an end to these affronts.

The railway reached Northiam in 1900 and closed 54 years later because it did not pay. The early London commuters would walk, or run, the 1½ miles from the village to the station to catch the 7am train up to town. Sometimes they arrived too late, but more often than not their absence was noted and the train would stop and come back for them. Easy-going days, those, when the passengers were allowed to get off at the station and pick bunches of flowers before being chivvied back aboard when the train was about to depart.

A carrier nicknamed Hard Times used to drive to Rye to pick up the mail and bring it back to the village. He livened up his return journey with a glass or two which led to a little song from the children:

> 'Have you seen old Hard Times
> Coming home from Rye,
> First he calls at Peace and Plenty,
> Then at Hare and Hounds,
> Then the Cock and Old Jemima,
> Then the Rose and Crown.'

John Frewen, a sturdy puritan who became rector in 1558, baptised his first two sons Accepted and Thankful, perhaps in recognition of his appointment. Accepted pursued a glittering academic career and was made Archbishop of York in 1660.

The time-battered oak on the village green is the spot where Queen Elizabeth I stopped on her way to Rye and enjoyed a meal made by George Bishop and his family from Hayes Farm. The Virgin Queen left Northiam with a lasting memento of her brief stop – her green damask shoes. She changed into a pair worn by one of her hand maids (it is not recorded how the poor girl managed to continue on the royal progress).

Four Prime Ministers gathered on the playing field in May 1944 for a final inspection of the troops of Southern Command before D Day. Their names were recorded on the gates erected by the parish to commemorate the visit: Rt Hon. Winston S. Churchill (Great Britain), Rt Hon. Mackenzie King (Canada), Rt Hon. Field Marshall Jan Christian Smuts (South Africa) and the Hon. Sir Godfrey M. Huggins (Southern Rhodesia).

Travelling fairs were held on the green and in the field behind The Crown and Thistle, and on the frequent visits of the circus it was customary to cause a little consternation by letting lion cubs loose among the crowds. The Crown and Thistle was the destination of the all-male Northiam Slate Club on their procession through the village on the first Thursday in May wearing white smocks and bowler hats. At the pub they had bread and cheese, and then it was on to the green where dinner was served in a tent.

This ceased in 1904. Gone too is the Summer Cycle Parade with lavishly decorated bicycles, and the spring visit to homes by youngsters carrying a flower-decked maypole and chanting:

'Penny, penny poppy show.
Give me a penny I'll let you see'

The St Francis Hospital for animals flourishes at Northiam on land given to the Sussex Blue Cross Branch of Our Dumb Friends League by Miss Kitty Comport in memory of her father and brother. The first residents were two donkeys, Aunt Rose and Midge.

There are few tales of ghosts in the village despite its great age, but former organist Mr Holdstock had two strange experiences while practising in the church. He heard men's voices in the vestry though he knew no-one was there and the outer door was locked; and on another occasion when he was playing there came the strong fragrance of Arum Lilies, though there were no flowers to account for the heady scent.

The jubilee of Queen Victoria in 1897 was marked in a practical if strange way by the purchase of a Pony and Hand Hearse, made by Mr H. Kemp of Hawkhurst for £27. Funerals were conducted with it until recent years. The hearse, a magnificently ornate affair, has found its own final resting place at the village's

Perigoe Workshop Museum.

All garden lovers or people who study pretty pictures on calendars will have heard of Great Dixter, with its beautiful grounds and timber-framed medieval house. It was bought by Mr Nathanial Lloyd in 1910 and he employed Mr Edwin Lutyens (later the architect of New Delhi, for which he was knighted) for restoration and additions. One day the pair were driving through Benenden in Kent when they saw a derelict 16th century hall about to be pulled down. It had a seedy past and was known as 'The Old House at Home.' Mr Lloyd bought it, the timbers were numbered joint by joint and it was brought to Great Dixter and reassembled as part of the additions on the south side.

Northiam is the birthplace of the Sussex Scone, larger than the usual variety and incorporating cinnamon and honey among other things in the old recipe. Pat and Brian Cutler, who make them, sold more than 7,500 in the space of six months, with visitors to Great Dixter accounting for a large proportion.

Nutley

It has something of the feel of a frontier town in the Wild West, on a smaller scale of course. Straddling the old turnpike road from East Grinstread to Lewes, its people used to eke out their livings on Ashdown Forest, which still stretches unkempt and sometimes forbidding up to the cottage gardens.

It was a rough and ready kind of place in the old days. The Sussex historian Mark Antony Lower denounced forest dwellers as rogues and vagabonds '... the locality was infamous ... for the deeds of poachers, horse stealers and smugglers.'

When the fair visited Nutley, in the field by the old Shelley Arms, the stallholders always nailed their gingerbread to the counter for fear the 'foresty people' would snatch the lot.

A unique record of the village's past was made by Arthur Francis, known to everyone as 'Daddy', in a collection of photographs taken at the turn of the century, not only portraits of people but of the buildings and local activities, building-up a panoramic picture of the parish. There were many more forest dwellings than there are now and also industries which have disappeared like hop growing and brick making.

The writer Barbara Willard, who lives in the village, records the 'strange ragged characters under rough shelters, barefooted children, bearded tinkers. There was great poverty and loneliness, even so short a time ago. The road was small, dusty and winding; and at the pub on the corner, one that has now gone, the landlord would give you a pint of beer just to stay and talk to him.'

Today's residents are more affluent and the sense of pride they have in their village is reflected in the hassocks in the church, made by the locals and all beautifully decorated, some with forest themes.

Nutley has always been renowned for the prowess of its stool-ball teams, the game said to have been invented by milkmaids using their milking stools as bats that Sussex has made her own, and for its formidable tug-of-war team.

It has also become something of a mecca for Red Indian enthusiasts, people whose interest in the North American tribes extends to wearing eagle feather bonnets, buckskin, beads and moccasins; setting up teepees and singing and dancing in true redskin style. The local devotees are Peter 'Badger' Kirby and his wife Dawn who put on displays for good causes (and entertainment) and in May play hosts at what has become an annual 'pow wow' of fellow Indian devotees at the village hall. They come from all over Europe in their finery and add more than a touch of colour to village life.

A Wellington bomber crashed near here in July, 1941, after a raid over Germany. A memorial to Sgt. Pilot Victor Ronald Sutton was erected at the site, now given a wall made of local stone. It is known locally as the "airmen's grave" though none of the plane's crew is actually buried here. The inscription reads: "To the glorious memory of Sgt/P. V.R. Sutton, aged 24 years, 142 Bom. Sqdn. RAF also his five comrades who lost their lives through enemy action 31-7-41. Mother." Every Remembrance Sunday the Conservators of Ashdown Forest are among those who lay a wreath at the site.

Nutley's wooden windmill, the open trestle post variety, ceased its commercial life in 1908 but has been lovingly restored by members of the Uckfield and District Preservation Society for

which they gained a European Architectural Heritage Year Award in 1975. Today it is claimed to be the oldest working windmill in Sussex.

It is to the forest that the village owes the local legend of the headless ghost. A smuggler had his head shot off in a fight with the preventive men and his spirit wanders the lonely hills and valleys with a lantern, supposedly searching for the spot where he hid his kegs of brandy before coming to such an unfortunate end at the hands of the King's men.

Offham 🌿

Pronounced 'Oaf-ham', it is a village in miniature: A fine country house or two and no more than a handful of pretty flint cottages served by a handsome church, a pub and even a blacksmith's forge where the toil of days gone by has given way to more artistic creations in metal. A sleepy place where the locals plead for a crossing, to make a walk across the busy main road less perilous, and lament the loss of their village shop.

But the industrial revolution once hit Offham in a big way making it the scene of a remarkable piece of engineering and one of the first "railways" in southern England.

At the beginning of the 19th century George Shiffner, who lived at Coombe Place, owned the village's chalk pit and wanted to improve on the horse and cart method of transporting the chalk and lime down the steep hillside to the canal in the Ouse valley 400ft below. Shiffner commissioned William Jessop to solve the problem and in 1809 the Offham tramway was opened operating on a funicular basis.

The loaded wagons were attached to cables and rolled on rails down a 1 in 2 gradient controlled by a large wheel at the top which simultaneously pulled up an empty wagon on the adjacent track. The wagons descended and ascended through two brick tunnels 7ft wide which passed under the road below the chalk pit. At the bottom the wagons were put on a turntable, disgorged their burden into the waiting barge and were pulled up again.

As the conventional railways arrived the waterway traffic diminished, but the Offham tramway continued to hump its loads until closure in 1870 and traces of the mechanical era which made the village buzz with activity can still be seen today.

Old Heathfield 🌿

They like to make sure you stick on the 'old' in these parts because the inhabitants of the original community like to preserve their independence from the bustling and rapidly expanding market town which grew with the railway. Old Heathfield is separated from its younger but larger brother by Heathfield Park, which is surrounded by a high stone wall three miles long; it took an old workman three years to build it single-handed – and at a mile a year that is not bad going.

In the mansion at Heathfield Park lived General George Augustus Elliott, Baron Heathfield, who successfully defended Gibraltar against the Spanish in a siege lasting three years in the 18th century. The Gibraltar Tower in the grounds of the park was erected in his memory. Standing 55 feet high, the visitor is supposed to be able to see 40 churches from the top, given a clear day (and a telescope).

George Gilbert, one-time soldier, obtained work in Heathfield on the estate of his old commander. He became a travelling Methodist preacher, and his powerful oratory was heard in villages throughout the county, though not always listened to. At Ticehurst they pelted him with mud and stones while the church bells were rung to drown his words.

With a wife and 10 children to support through carpentry, he eventually received a stipend of £28 a year and a tiny vegetable patch which allowed him to devote himself to preaching. He even managed to save £200, which he lent to a friend and never got back. His wife was distraught at the news, but Gilbert was stoic: 'Look up, dame; bring me my pipe,' was his response to the family misfortune. He died in 1827 at the ripe old age of 87.

Here, too, Jonathan Harmer plied his rather macabre trade in the 19th century. He was a sculptor who specialised in terracotta plaques for tombstones. Harmer plaques come in seven main varieties including baskets of fruit and flowers, urns with horn handles and figure groups representing Faith, Hope and Charity. They come in various colours, too, the red versions originating from a local claypit and the paler creams and buffs from further afield. At the Cade Street Independent Chapel are two particularly interesting wall tablets of an urn with swags, one inscribed 'Harmer fecit 1832', the other 'Harmer 1878'. It must have been taken from stock for the craftsman died 29 years earlier!

It is many years since there has been a Heathfield (or Heffle to give it the right pronunciation) Fair. They were held on April 14 at Cade Street, the day everyone in Sussex, no matter where they happen to be, can legitimately say they have heard the first cuckoo of summer: Because at Heffle Fair an old woman was said to release the bird from her basket. They seem to have been lively events, with plenty of stock and a strong gipsy horse-trading element. Local people used to have gates which opened outwards, to stop wayward animals barging their way into the gardens.

Heathfield contradicts Shakespeare in asserting that Jack Cade, leader of the 15th century rebellion that bears his name, died in a garden here and not in Kent where the bard places it.

126

Cade had gone into hiding at Newick Farm, at Heathfield, and ventured out one evening to play bowls at the inn. He was discovered and shot with an arrow by Alexander Iden, Sheriff of Kent, his body being taken to London and his head fixed to a pike on London Bridge. A pillar at Cade Street commemorates the event and states: 'This is the success of all rebels, and this fortune chanceth ever to traitors.'

A reminder of a more serene past is Turner's Vale of Heathfield, perhaps the best of the artist's many works in Sussex. The view is still very much as he saw it nearly two centuries ago.

Ovingdean

Historians shake their heads firmly at the suggestion that Charles II rested at the manor house after his escape from Worcester and before embarking for the Continent from Shoreham. The tradition is a strong one, though, and one scribe cites a letter written to Sir William Burrell in 1780 relating how the fugitive King's stalwart appearance 'had such an effect upon the good woman of the house that her next child (a very fine boy) was said to be the picture of the King.'

Seaside suburbia has not strangled a hamlet immortalised by Harrison Ainsworth in his novel *Ovingdean Grange,* where he writes glowingly about the charms of the part Saxon church. Not surprisingly, it is adorned like so many others by a window by Charles Eamer Kempe, whose family lived at Ovingdean and who was buried here in 1907.

Peasmarsh

When landlord Mick Pithie left the Horse and Cart at Peasmarsh he decided to give his old regulars a treat. They were all invited to the opening night of his new pub, The Curlew at Hurst Green. It promised to be a highly alcoholic affair and to avoid his former customers falling foul of drinking and driving Mr Pithie laid on a London double-decker bus to get them all there and back safely.

A responsible approach which, according to Mark Antony Lower in *The Worthies of Sussex* (1865) was seriously lacking in a son of Peasmarsh from an earlier age. William Pattison was born here in 1706, a gifted poet who while at school built up debts amounting to £10 with booksellers. With the creditors getting fiercer and no money in his pockets, Pattison literally wrote himself out of trouble by penning *An Ode on Christmas Day* and inscribing it to Sir Christopher Musgrave of Edenhall. He then introduced himself to the baronet who was so pleased with the ode that he immediately paid off all the debts.

Pattison got to Cambridge where, in today's parlance, he seems to have had 'the wrong attitude.' He was threatened with expulsion but left of his own accord and set himself up as a professional poet. He was soon homeless and starving in London and died of smallpox at the age of 21. Lower laments: 'with abilities of a high order, he had no steadiness of purpose, or depth of principle. From the extreme licentiousness of his poetry the world was a gainer by his death, and Sussex can take little credit to herself for having given him birth. Most of his poems were written before he was nineteen and they show a moral depravity quite remarkable for that early period of life.'

Strong stuff! But by the standards of the 20th century the schoolboy poet's work is unlikely to raise any shocked eyebrows at all.

Peasmarsh church lies well away from the rest of the village, giving rise to theories of an earlier community being wiped out by the Black Death. It stands serene among meadows and nearby is Peasmarsh Place, former home of the Liddell family who had several claims to fame. The Very Rev H.G. Liddell was Dean of Christ Church, Oxford; his son Edward was a joint compiler of Liddell and Scott's Greek Dictionary (on the bookshelf of every classicist); and his daughter Alice persuaded a friend of his to tell her a story. The friend was the Rev Charles Dodgson (Lewis Carroll) and the story was *Alice's Adventures in Wonderland.*

Penhurst 🪶

The loneliest place in the county. Even people who profess to have a knowledge of Sussex have never heard of it. In loneliness lies beauty. Penhurst is a church, a manor house and a few farm buildings; a living picture of old England that has scarcely changed since Shakespeare's day. The hairpin lanes that shield it from the rest of the world are calculated to cut it off completely during the winter.

In the Elizabethan manor house are the last three firebacks cast at the last furnace of the Sussex iron industry at neighbouring Ashburnham. The man who did the job before the fire was extinguished for good in 1813 has been recorded for posterity. He was Will Rummins according to a former rector of Penhurst, the Rev R.W. Whistler, who was given the name by the last labourer at Ashburnham Furnace, William Hobday who died in August 1883.

Joseph Wise, rector for 46 years until his death in 1810, managed to maintain a family of nine children on a stipend of £100 per annum. He supplemented his income by publishing a number of books, including an *Ode on the marriage of George III and Queen*.

A little ingenuity keeps the congregation comfortable in the winter when hot air is pumped into the church by an agricultural corn drier. The old copper lamp at the entrance to the churchyard strikes an even more incongruous note; it once lit the streets of Clerkenwell in London.

In an area of such solitude the 20th century can be left behind and it is easy to believe the legend that in the sinister-sounding Creep Wood the Britons made a last stand in a desperate battle against the Saxons.

Pett 🪶

It gives its name to the stretch of marshland that runs from the village to Winchelsea. Wild and none too attractive. A bit like the eccentric brothers Daniel and Edward Thurston, who lived here

The brothers occupied a tumbledown shack on the foreshore at Pett Level and travelled the area in a pony and trap specialising in mending leather bellows. Old, unkempt and peculiar, they were given the cold shoulder by many of the locals and their shack, made from an old boat and driftwood, became known as Uncle Tom's Cabin.

The Thurstons would supplement their income with a little fishing and they kept a few sheep on the free marshland. But it was not enough to keep them out of debt. *Sussex Life* recorded that one night local farmers cornered the brothers in their cabin demanding payment for hay and feed. One of the Thurstons tore a patch from his jacket, stuffed it into his pipe and lit up. The resultant stench in the confined space put all the creditors to flight.

A folly on the grand scale ends at Pett. The Royal Military Canal, running from Cliff End to Shorncliffe in Kent, was conceived as a sort of moat to keep out the French invaders. It cost Pitt's government £200,000 but was barely finished before the craziness of the operation became apparent; that an army that had crossed Europe's great rivers (not to mention the English Channel) would be thwarted by a canal barely 30 feet wide. It is a pleasant spot for walking though, and must have provided plenty of employment in its time.

The evils of the demon drink cost villagers their pub for a period of about 70 years. The Royal Oak Inn was closed by landowner Mrs Lucal Shadwell, of Fairlight, in whose estate it was included. It was at the annual tenants' ball at the big house that the behaviour of some of her Pett tenants upset her; they were having too much of a good time it seems, so she turned the pub into a temperance hotel and the sale of liquor was banned. Trade soon fell away but there was no relenting and the village stayed 'dry' for a generation and more. Happily, alcoholic beverages can be bought at the bar today.

The Department of Trade had to get tough with unofficial salvage teams and souvenir hunters attracted in 1974 by the wreck of the Anne, a British frigate lying in the sands off Pett Level. They were threatened with a maximum fine of £400 for tampering with the vessel, which was beached on the coast and burnt by her captain after a battle off Beachy Head between the British and Dutch fleets and the French fleet in 1690.

Pevensey

'Lookers', men employed to keep an eye on a farmer's animals as they grazed and ensure that none went astray or were stolen, are a breed of the past. It took a special kind of character to endure the hours of solitude in all weathers, but at Pevensey Horace Field made up for it when he returned to human company. He was the last looker of the marshes, with a great beard as white as the wool on the sheep he tended. His day's work done, Horace would invariably make his way to the local hostelry where he was renowned as a demon at dominoes.

William of Normandy landed here with his mighty invasion fleet in 1066, though he was not the first conqueror to come to Pevensey. The Romans built the original fortress of Anderida which was added to down the centuries to become the pride of the village, with walls 12ft thick and 25ft high enclosing an area of about 10 acres.

It has had a bloody history. In 490 AD it was besieged by Aella the Saxon, who slaughtered all the British inhabitants; it withstood a siege by Simon de Montfort; and in 1399 Lady Pelham defended it against the Yorkists. Twenty years later Queen Joanna, widow of Henry IV, was imprisoned in the castle for four years by her stepson on a charge of witchcraft. Her custody under Sir John Pelham can't have been too uncomfortable for she was allowed nine servants.

During the reign of Elizabeth I the castle was ordered to be razed to the ground, though the command was ignored, and in 1650 it was sold to a builder for £40 as a pile of stones. He obviously did not think it was worth the demolition job. In 1940 it was ready for a German invasion, with reinforced towers and pill boxes disguised as ancient masonry.

The sea which made Pevensey an important strategic centre had retreated long before the Second World War, leaving the village more than a mile inland. Evidence of that former greatness as a medieval commercial centre lies in the coins which have survived from the days when it had its own mint. The much restored Mint House stands in the single street of cobble and flint, along with the Court House, reputed to be the smallest town hall in England in the days when Pevensey had its own mayor and corporation.

There is a story of one mayor busily thatching his pigsty one day when a messenger arrived with an important letter. The mayor adopted an important air and put on his spectacles, broke the seal of the document and began to read it upside down. The messenger politely suggested that it would be easier if he held it the right way up, and was told: 'Hold your tongue, sir, for while I am mayor of Pevensey I'll hold a letter which end uppards I like!'

The village court once found a man guilty of manslaughter because he stole a pair of buckskin breeches – the theft was a capital one and so the jurers hastily looked for a sentence which carried something less than the death penalty. They used to have a nasty way of executing felons, incidentally – by drowning them.

The court house also served as the village lock-up, and one of the last people to be incarcerated there was Betty Breach. Her husband Billy had a frequent thirst and had lingered too long in the New Inn one night. So she went to retrieve him, emptied the remainder of his drink over his head and smashed the glass under her feet. For this she was jailed by a zealous magistrate, who relented when he saw public opinion was against him and sent word that the prison door be opened. Stubborn Betty refused to leave until the magistrate came in person to let her out and apologise. He did, and she went home to her spouse in triumph.

The Breach family also caused a stir one Christmas Day, when the sound of raised voices was heard from their cottage and the window pane suddenly shattered under the impact of a plum pudding which came to rest in the street. Billy had apparently paid another lengthy visit to the pub.

Andrew Borde, whose bubbly personality earned him the nickname Merry Andrew, a phrase which has passed into the English language, lived for some time at Pevensey. This one time Carthusian friar, scholar and physician to Henry VIII seems to have advertised his healing powers by shouting them to all and sundry at country fairs. For all his cheeky-chappie image with the fairground crowds he remained a monk at heart, staying celibate, drinking only water three times a week, wearing a hair shirt and hanging his shroud at the foot of his bed every night. He wrote a great deal, from *The Principles of Astronomical Prognostications* to the more racy *Merry Tales of the Mad Men of Gotham*.

To the east lie Pevensey Levels, which may look like empty and windswept acres stretching as far as the eye can see and broken by countless dykes, but are to the naturalist a place of great importance as a habitat for rare flora and fauna. The levels end at the shoreline, where less than a century ago the natives still walked with 'backsters', flat pieces of wood fastened to the soles of their boots to enable them to get across the pebbles.

Here were erected the Martello Towers, 40 feet high and of such a thickness they required 50,000 bricks to complete a single course, to withstand the threatened Napoleonic invasion of England. Behind these forts the stalwarts of Pevensey were ready to deal with the French too. A song of the time ran:

> 'If Bonyparte should have the heart,
> To land on Pemsey Level,
> Then my three sons with their three guns
> Would blow him to the devil.'

Piddinghoe

> 'Englishmen fight, French 'uns too,
> We don't, we live Piddinghoe'

A rhyme that originated from the insular and independent nature of the village in the old days, perhaps, or simply a way of making sure the 'furriners' got the pronunciation of the name right.

Certainly in the smuggling days Piddinghoe folk would want to keep themselves to themselves. Set beside the river Ouse just three miles from the sea, this village was in an ideal position to prosper from contraband. The quantity of illicit spirits hidden in pits here and removed at night gave rise to the proverbs: 'At Piddinghoe they dig for moonshine'; 'At Piddinghoe they dig for smoke'; and 'At Piddinghoe they dig for daylight.'

An industry of the past gave rise to yet another anecdote – that the natives 'hang the ponds out to dry.' They made whiting here by grinding chalk in water. When this had been allowed to drain the sediment was dug out and put on shelves to dry.

Another source of employment which has long since disappeared was the brickworks, and in the grounds of Kiln Cottage is the only remaining bottle-shaped kiln in the county. It was last used just before the First World War, but in 1980 was dismantled and painstakingly rebuilt.

The ebb and flow of the river, with its majestic curve around the cluster of old cottages, plays just as big a part in the life of the village today as it did in the era of the smuggling brethren. Villagers cannot escape the assortment of craft which pass up and down or the more eccentric events for which the Ouse is famous. Piddinghoe is the finishing line for a plastic duck race from Southease Bridge.

Hundreds of ducks (the conventional bath variety) are tipped into the water to leisurely float down to the finish, though the majority make a beak-line for the banks. The Southern Water Authority gives permission for the race with the following stipulations: No duck over 6ft should attempt to negotiate beneath Southease Bridge; and no duck should exceed the speed limit of five knots.

Piddinghoe church is one of only three in Sussex with a round tower built of flint, all of them being in the Ouse valley (the others are at Southease and St Michael's in Lewes). The theory is that they were designed to be used as a series of beacon towers. In 1980 the lofty heights of Piddinghoe's church were scaled in order for the weathervane to be repaired – a vane immortalised by Kipling in his poem *Sussex*: 'Where windy Piddinghoe's begilded dolphin veers'. The locals will tell you that it is not a dolphin at all, but a salmon trout.

When little Edith Croft died in 1868 at the age of three months, her grandmother launched a fund which perpetuates the little girl's memory to this day. The endowment of £100 was to be known as Little Edith's Treat and was to be spent on her birthday on July 19th. The bequest still provides an income which goes towards a treat for the village children.

Piltdown

The skull on the inn sign has been painted wearing a wicked leer; the sort of skull, if that is possible, that appreciates a joke. The joke made the name of this scattered hamlet ring round the world and fooled the experts for years.

The skull of Dawn Man, almost the missing link, was unearthed at Piltdown in 1912 and acclaimed as the finest primitive relic ever discovered in England. It was found by Charles Dawson, a solicitor and geologist from Lewes, when some workmen were digging for gravel – they had apparently thought the fragment of cranium was a piece of coconut. The Lamb Inn adopted the skull as its sign and became the Piltdown Man. The scene of the discovery became a place of pilgrimage, and Dawson was feted for his major breakthrough. Only the passage of time revealed that it was all a hoax, that the skull belonged to a monkey and that Mr Dawson either planted it and went laughing to his grave or was himself the victim of deception.

Maybe there is something in the Piltdown air that prompts a leg-pull. In far more recent times an American gentleman wrote to the local newspaper asking of anyone else had witnessed what he had seen: A pterodactyl flapping its way leisurely over Piltdown Golf Course.

A section of the golf course is said to cover a 'plague pit', where the unfortunate local victims of the Black Death were buried in a mass grave, though others say the site is near the village stores. A happier place is Piltdown Pond, more of a lake really, a popular spot for anglers and duck fanciers.

Playden

Rather overshadowed by Rye, only half-a-mile to the south, but fiercely proud of the fact that it was once held to be more important. Pleidenam occupies a distinct place in the Domesday Book, whereas Rye at that time was only part of Rameslie under the Manor of Brede.

It was suggested that the county highways department should

celebrate this fact by putting up special road signs proclaiming the village's antiquity on the 900th anniversary of Domesday.

Like an upright citizen with skeletons in the closet, proud Playden once had another name, and a shadier past. Long ago, when the men of the village were still close enough to the receding sea to catch cod they would salt the fish and spread them on the roadside banks to dry, earning the name Salcot or Sauket Street. An old proverb asserts:

> 'Sauket church, crooked steeple,
> Drunken parson, wicked people.'

The man in charge of the leper hospital here in 1379 seems to have been the sort of rogue this sweeping condemnation of the population was aimed at. Robert de Burton was said to have 'made waste, sale, destruction and dilapidation of the Hospital and its goods, to the final destruction of it.' He was also accused of felling oaks for his own profit and of selling corn which was meant for the benefit of the poor.

In later years Playden's wicked people seem to have mellowed. When Robert Walker could not afford to comply with the Act of 1678 and bury his daughter Anne in woollen cloth his £5 penalty was paid by Thomas Rogeres and John Duke, according to the church records.

A Flemish brewer was buried here in 1530, his trade denoted by the two casks and a crossed mashstick and fork ornamenting the black stone slab in the north aisle. The incised drawings were once inlaid with brass.

Plumpton 🐛

Even a confirmed teetotaller could find himself seeing double at the Half Moon. Many of the pub's regulars are recorded in a giant painting which takes pride of place in the bar, raising their glasses in a cheery salute to the beholder. Landlord Terry White commissioned the unusual work of art as a tribute to his customers and it was completed over a nine-month period in 1979 by Sussex portrait painter Dick Leech. More than 100 local folk are depicted at their favourite haunt in what Mr White described as 'an historical document.'

Such a communal kind of immortality would not have pleased a Plumpton resident of earlier generations. Old Martha, a strange, witch-like old lady from the 19th century, had a morbid fear of being photographed for posterity by euthusiasts in search of village oddities (she was eventually captured on film from the safety of a shrubbery).

Old Martha was reputedly 100 years old and held in awe by all who knew her, believing she had the power of good and evil and could cast spells. She lived in a hovel but was reputed to be rich, with houses and land of her own. She made no secret of the fact that somewhere she had hidden a bagful of golden guineas. Dressed in outlandish attire she would tramp the countryside for miles singing and dancing as she went and ringing little bells. Despite her great age she was as nimble and fast as a hare, into which it was maintained she would change on occasion. She would cover great distances with an enormous basket under her arm, often running backwards. A journey over the Downs to

Brighton, where she was a familiar character picking up many pounds through the practice of her magic arts, was commonplace. The secret of the golden guineas, by the way, died with the old eccentric.

Gold of another kind is associated with Plumpton Place, a half-timbered Tudor house surrounded by a moat and the most impressive building in this pretty but scattered Downland village. During the reign of Henry VIII, Sir Leonard Mascall is said to have introduced golden carp and golden pippins to England here. According to an old proverb:

'Turkeys, carp, hops, pickerel and beer,
Came into England all in one year.'

The illustrious Sir Leonard seems to have held an important post in the household of the Archbishop of Canterbury. He is called 'clerk of the kitchen', presumably a kind of steward. In his own home he appears to have been something of an experimental farmer, with flocks and herds that grazed on the Downs above his house, and he wrote many books from ... *the Arte and manner howe to plant and graffe all sortes of trees, howe to set stons and soewe Pepines, to make wild trees graft on* to how to *take spots and staines out of Silks, Velvets and Linen, and Woollen Clothes.* Not riveting titles, perhaps, but he was a best-seller long before Shakespeare got into print.

John Dudeney, the shepherd who became a schoolmaster, lived with his grandfather at Plumpton as a boy at a house now identified as The Cottage, across the road from the Half Moon. No doubt he would climb up to lofty Plumpton Plain to help trap wheatears to sell in the towns. They were a great delicacy in the 18th century and nicknamed The English Ortolan. The numbers snared 'amounted annually to about one thousand eight hundred and forty dozen'. No wonder the wheatear soon became a rarity!

Plumpton Green

Picturesque it isn't. Some would even dispute its right to be described as a village in its own right. But its people stick up fiercely for this appendage to the far more historic community of Plumpton, two miles down the road, and it is interesting to see how such a comparatively new rural community can swiftly establish a sense of identity.

Plumpton Green grew up beside the railway station, swiftly acquiring all the virtues of mid-Victorian country life: spacious villas, a church (unusual in that it has an octagonal tower) and a school built in 1878 to replace the miniature schoolroom which Plumpton had built in 1837. The first headmaster of the new establishment must have been a rather awesome figure who certainly commanded respect.

Daddy Batchelor, as he was known, was recalled in 1974 when the school was about to be superseded by a new, antiseptic structure. The Victorian scholars' jingle to their mentor was chanted at a special open day:

> 'Old Daddy Batchelor's a nice old man,
> He tries to teach us all he can,
> Read, write and arithmetic,
> He never forgets to give us the stick.
> When he does, he makes us dance,
> Out of England into France,
> Out of France into Spain,
> Over the hills and back again.'

Mr Raymond Woods was one of many locals who share happy memories of schooldays in Plumpton Green. On Ascension Day it became traditional for the youngsters to walk two miles for a service at St Michaels in Plumpton, then climb to The Cross on the Downs for a sandwich lunch. The afternoon would be spent below Black Cap 'sliding down the hillside on our bottoms.'

The Cross, incidentally, is only visible in the early morning or evening when the sun casts the right shadow. A plaque at the site maintains that it marks the site of the Battle of Lewes in 1264. This seems highly unlikely so far to the west, and locals have a more plausible story; that the cross was a guide for Crusaders heading for the coast on the long journey to fight in the Holy Land.

With the building of the National Hunt racecourse, Plumpton

Green has become a hive of activity on race days and at the end of the Second World War the village was agog at the prospect of an even greater claim to fame: as the site of London's new airport. How this rather ridiculous rumour came to be established is unknown, but it gradually faded away as did the wartime airfield to the north of the village for which such grandiose plans were said to be in the pipeline. The hasty building of the airfield had necessitated the demolition of a pub. Happily, The Plough was resurrected on a new site.

Ringmer

A place that has expanded so much in recent years that it ranks among the biggest villages in the county. But it is more than just a dormitory at the end of the working day for those that toil at the nearby county town of Lewes. Its people have a strong community spirit and nobody is allowed to forget one of Ringmer's most distinguished residents. He was Timothy the Tortoise, who takes pride of place on the village sign beside the green. He belonged to Mrs Rebecca Snooke, who lived at Delves House and was the aunt of the naturalist Gilbert White who took a great interest in the pet's habits when he paid visits.

White recorded: 'I was much taken with its sagacity in discerning those that do it kind offices; for as soon as the good old lady comes in sight who has waited on it for more than 30 years it hobbles towards its benefactress with awkward alacrity, but remains inattentive to strangers.

'Thus not only the ox knoweth its owner, and the ass his master's crib, but the most abject reptile and torpid of beings distinguishes the hand that feeds it, and is touched with the feelings of gratitude.'

In April 1780 the aged Timothy went to live with White at Selborne in Hampshire, being carried the 80 miles in post chaises which apparently perked him up enough to do two laps of the garden when he arrived. After the demise of the pet his shell was preserved at the British Museum.

Two Ringmer girls were married to famous men. John Sadler, vicar from 1620 to 1640, had a daughter who married John Harvard, founder of the university in America; and the daughter of Sir William Springett of Broyle Place, Gulielma Maria Posthuma (because she was born after his death in 1643) married William Penn, the Quaker who founded Pennsylvania.

Centrepiece of Ringmer is the village green, fringed (like all good greens) by old cottages and the parish church of St Mary which dates mainly from the 14th century and has had a singularly unlucky time with its tower.

The first tower burned down in the mid 16th century and the second suffered the same fate in about 1800. The present tower was built in 1884 by William Martin, who is also credited with having made the first cycle in England with wooden wheels.

In the churchyard is the Butcher's Stone, not as sinister as the name might suggest but simply the place where the village butcher used to sharpen his knives, and a low stone building with a Horsham slab roof.

It looks as old as the church, but in fact dates back only as far as 1922 and was erected to bring music to the church in Heath Robinson (but effective) style.

When the villagers acquired a new organ soon after the First World War it was far too big to be pumped by hand and there was no electricity to do the job. So the new building went up to house a motorcycle engine and a fan which blew air through an underground duct to the organ in the church. Electricity has now replaced the old engine but you can still hear the fan at work if you stand outside when the organ is playing.

One of the most devout churchgoers in the parish was Herbert Springett, whose determination to be punctual for church must have been a curious sight in 17th century Ringmer. When the roads were too muddy for his horses he yoked eight oxen to his carriage to be sure of getting to his destination on time.

Life must have been desperately tough in this area 150 years ago. The great mass of the people were attached to agriculture and when the winter came they were likely to be laid off. Ringmer found an answer to feeding the men and their families who had little or no money coming in during the harsh weather by establishing a soup kitchen, used by two-thirds of the population twice a week. Local man John Kay discovered the following soup recipe for 1839 scribbled in the margin of a memorandum book for the period: 'Half bushel carrots, six gallons turnips, four gallons onions, 3lb Scotch barley, four gallons peas, 70lb beef, half head, 10lb oatmeal, 7lb salt, 6ozs pepper, 560 loaves bread.'

With the services of two cooks, the bill for that sea of soup amounted to £3.10s.11d (£3.55) a time. Mr Kay said: 'Attached to the recipe was a list of those who received it – 207 families, containing 379 adults and 544 children. In total about 923 people, or two-thirds of the Ringmer population of the time.'

The soup looks nutritious enough (perhaps not a lot when divided among nearly 1,000 people) but the recipients would not be used to much of anything. It is certainly a sobering reminder that Ringmer has not always been the prosperous place that it is today.

On the Green, in November 1830, 150 farm labourers met Lord Gage to complain about the enclosures of common field land which had reduced them from extreme poverty to starvation and from independence to serfdom. They asked for their wages to be increased from 9d to 2/6 per day and for the dismissal of the cruel Poor Law Overseers, particularly the one in Ringmer whom they described as 'lost to all feelings of humanity'. Lord Gage agreed to their requests and the men dispersed 'with hymns and tears of joy', stopping on the way to smash the village grindstone which symbolised their suffering.

One Horace Theophilus King, known to everyone as Alf, was an old craftsman famous within living memory for his thatched cornstacks with little plaited straw crowns. He also had a powerful regard for the old Sussex saying 'We won't be druv.'

To demonstrate that the Green was common land to all Ringmer people he sat down in the centre of the cricket pitch while a match was in progress and refused to budge. The old timer took no notice of the pleas, arguments or threats and eventually had to be carried off. An early example of the sit down protest.

Another local of the old days with something of a stubborn streak was the village sweep, who tethered his pony in the church porch, claiming he had as much right to do so as a certain well-to-do lady who did the same with her pet dog when she went to services. The sweep apparently got short shrift from the vicar.

On the road to Laughton is a large wooden building, now hunt kennels but in the early years of the last century the Ringmer lunatic asylum. It must have been a grim place for in 1853 the Commissioners in Lunacy made an adverse report on it and it closed down two years later.

The building had served as a barracks for officers stationed in the village during the Napoleonic Wars, with the other ranks a little way off at Rushey Green.

Here two of the soldiers fought a duel and killed each other. The mounds of their graves can still be seen near the entrance to Plashett Park Farm.

Ringmer is a great sporting village (few who drive through can have failed to notice the flagpole on the Green surmounted by a cricket bat and ball), with soccer, bowls and even an annual run to the top of Mount Caburn and back.

In the Great War 28 out of the 34 playing members of the cricket club freely joined the colours. Those that did not return are remembered on a sad tribute in the church: 'They played the game.'

The soccer club reached a pinnacle in 1971 when they battled through to the first round proper of the FA Cup in true Boy's Own style. With the whole village (and most of Sussex) rooting for this mouse that roared the 'blue boys' were knocked out, honourably, by Colchester United from the Third Division.

Ripe 🌿

Scores of people remember The Great Omi, but once seen he was not the sort of man you could easily forget. This bizarre character, who claimed to be a member of an elephant-worshipping cult, had a face and body that were covered in stripes like a zebra.

The former public schoolboy and army officer, who lived with his wife in a caravan in a lonely wood in the parish, had a plastic surgeon slap dye under his skin to create the remarkable effect. He also sharpened his teeth to points and wore elephant teeth in his ears and a baby elephant's tusk in his nose. The Great Omi travelled the world with his wife (the Omette) and was a star of circus and stage from 1922 until the 1950s, the greatest tattoo attraction of his era. His appearance became more and more outrageous as the years went by, he took to wearing lipstick and nail polish and signed his pitch cards as the 'Barbaric Beauty.' He and his wife came to Ripe in their declining years, and certainly livened up the whole area.

Another eye-catcher in the village is a house, The Old Cottage, a timber framed building smothered in fantastic carvings: dolphins, cherubs, grotesque faces and patterns adorn the front. It dates from the 16th century and clearly not all the carving is contemporary. But some of it is believed to have come from Michelham Priory.

Ripe is small and undisturbed, well away from the main road and lying on the edge of the flatlands which finally rise to the south in the rolling curves of the Downs. It was referred to variously in the Domesday Book as Rype or Echentone, the second name living on in Eckington Manor, a chequer-brick early 18th century house.

In a village that has always been largely agricultural, and still is, it is nice to note that 500 years ago John Topyn left a cow, valued at 8s, to sustain the images of St John and St Dominic in the church.

The village is haunted by the ghost of a German pilot whose plane crashed here during the Second World War. A woman was driving along the lane near the scene of the crash one night when for no apparent reason everything in her car went dead, engine, lights, the lot. She looked out of the window and saw the phantom pilot sitting on a farm gate.

Robertsbridge

The name of the village is twinned with the Great English Game. The Gray-Nicholls factory has been making cricket bats here for more than a century, created from the finest willow grown at both local plantations and those further afield and hand-finished by the craftsmen at the rate of about 150 a day.

Some of the great names of cricket have wielded a Gray-Nicholls down the years, with England captain David Gower a more recent customer. The towering former Sussex and England captain Tony Greig took advantage of the factory's individual attention by having an extra long bat custom-made for him. Stoolball, a game almost exclusive to Sussex, is also catered for here by the manufacture of the round willow bats. The business moved in recent years to a site once occupied by another of the industries of the village – the toy factory where wooden playthings were made.

The Seven Stars at Robertsbridge has many claims on our attention. Built in 1194, it is reputed to be the oldest pub in the county, to have the longest curving bar counter (22 feet) and to have the largest single timber beam in Sussex (taken from the bottom of a ship).

It was a hostelry for the monks when they were building Robertsbridge Abbey and became an inn in 1380. It was here that the Abbot of Robertsbridge came to negotiate a deal for the release of King Richard the Lionheart, imprisoned in Austria, and later a tiny room at the inn is reputed to have been the hiding place of Charles II when Cromwell's roundheads were on his tail, though that particular monarch seems to have had hidey-holes the length and breadth of the county! There are ghosts, of course;

THE SEVEN STARS
ROBERTSBRIDGE

a monk in a red cloak who wanders the passageways, and a poltergeist who throws loaves of bread around the kitchen but who has quietened down considerably since being threatened by the landlady with exorcism.

Nothing much remains of the once noble abbey, just a few bits of refectory wall and various undercrofts which form part of the buildings of Abbey Farm, a private home. Although the abbey was not notorious, as were some other monastic houses, for laxity of morals and religion, instances are recorded illustrating that the monks did not always keep to the straight and narrow path. A royal pardon dated July 17, 1436 acquits the Abbot not only of all infringements of the statute law of which an upright man might unintentionally be guilty but also of 'all kinds of robberies, murders, rapes of women, rebellions, insurrections, felonies, conspiracies' etc, provided they were committed prior to September 2nd in the 10th year of Henry VI. It makes you wonder just what did go on at the old building.

The foundation stone of the Church Mission Room in the village was one of the bosses of the abbey roof. It seems to have been used as a common quarry after the Dissolution.

In the 13th century the King granted the Abbey the privilege of holding a fair from September 14th - 16th and a market on Mondays. The village once boasted two sites for these revelries, Upperfairfield and Le Bullocks fayrefield. Fairs continued to be held here until the middle of the present century, though the market had degenerated into a small fortnightly agricultural sale a hundred years before.

Robertsbridge is the village, but the tiny settlement of Salehurst half a mile away across the river Rother gives its name to the parish. In the stylish church, built of Hastings sandstone, is a 12th century font with a chain of salamanders (the emblem of a Crusader) crawling around the base of the shaft. It is claimed that Richard I gave the font to the church, though no real proof exists. Could it have been as a mark of gratitude to the Abbot for the part he played in securing the King's release?

The village used to be Rotherbridge, for obvious reasons, and a grim place Horace Walpole found it in 1752 when he paid a brief visit to this 'wretched village' over roads that 'grew bad beyond all badness.' He wrote in a letter of his arrival with a travelling friend: 'We had still six miles hither, but determined to stop as it would be a pity to break our necks before we had seen all we intended. But, alas! there was only one bed to be had: all the rest were inhabited by smugglers, whom the people of the house called mountebanks, and with one of whom the lady of the den told Mr Chute he might lie.' The travellers made their excuses and left.

The village fought long, hard and successfully to have a bypass to rid the pretty main street of the nerve-jarring stream of traffic on the A21, though a more peaceful road is the lane that leads to Brightling. At Darvell, once a TB sanitorium, is the headquarters of the Hutterian Society of Brothers, a community of men, women and children who hold everything in common and use no currency. Some 200 people live there, making wooden play equipment in the commune's workshop the income from which pays for their simple way of life. It has its own school and most of the clothes worn by the residents are made on the premises.

Rodmell ✣

The Mill on the Road is given as one source of the name; far more attractive than the basic 'Red-Mould' derived from the reddish tinge of the local ploughlands.

Certainly mills and millers have played their part in Rodmell's past, though there is no mill in the village today – just the memory of its site on the Downs in the name Mill Road. When the mill was demolished its timbers stayed on in the village, incorporated in the construction of a cottage.

Local folklore says that when the village blacksmith fashioned a new bell for the church tower it not only disturbed the slumbers of the windmiller but drove him to distraction. He cursed the church, the bell and the blacksmith, and finally in desperation sought the help of the village witch to end the clangour. She told him he could only stop the noise by tying a hair from the tail of the Devil to the bell's clapper. Not an easy item to come by, and the miller resigned himself to living with the racket.

Many years later the miller lost his way in a sea fog which enveloped the flooded flatlands of the Ouse below Rodmell.

Only by following the sound of the church bell was he able to find the ford which led to the village and avoid a watery grave. Filled with gratitude and contrition, he promptly presented the village with a new chime of bells.

In the churchyard, approached like the 12th century building itself, through the netball court of the village school, is the grave of the last miller of Rodmell, marked appropriately by a millstone. There is also a grave which tells the tragic tale of two lovers buried here 200 years ago. A young man died while trying to save a dog from drowning and the young woman died in her grief for him.

Virginia Woolf, the novelist and literary critic, lived in this peaceful place of flint and thatch for more than 20 years before making her final, sad journey to suicide in 1941 along the track which leads from the village street to the Ouse. Her husband Leonard lived on in Monk's House until his death and the property now belongs to the National Trust.

They are not too keen on change in this village. When Anthony and Susan Paice took over at The Holly in 1985 they were persuaded by the regulars to change the name back to the original Abergavenny Arms. 'We didn't think The Holly sounded right for a village inn 400 years old,' said Susan.

Rotherfield 🦡

Mutations in this pretty hilltop village? The women native to these parts were said to be unusually tall which gave rise to the belief that they were endowed with an extra pair of ribs.

A formidable female who ended her days here was Sophia Louisa Jex-Blake, who single-handedly opened up the medical profession to women. While in the United States in the 1860s she studied medicine and surgery and then sought to qualify in Britain as a doctor. But she found the doors of the London schools closed to her.

She launched the London School of Medicine for Women, within three years the Royal Free Hospital admitted her students to practice and in 1876 an Act was passed in Parliament enabling all medical examining bodies to include women candidates. A

148

year later Sophia was able to put up a sign as the first woman doctor in the country. She passed the last 12 years of a fruitful life in Rotherfield and died in 1912.

The story of the church is an interesting one. In the eighth century Berhtwald, Duke of the South Saxons was a sick man and, unable to find a cure at home, made a pilgrimage to an abbey in France where the bones of three saints where held to work miracles. One of the saints was Dionusius (or Denys) and it was perhaps these particular holy relics that effected Berhtwald's cure for on his return he founded the church here in 792 AD in honour of St Denys. In his will he threatened grim retribution on anyone attempting to usurp, defraud or curtail his gift.

The link with France that stetches back 1,200 years nearly became stronger when the parish council considered forming a twin-town relationship with St Denys near Paris, but the move foundered because it was decided the two communities were not compatible.

The laws of sanctuary probably saved two murderers from execution when they sought refuge in the church a century ago, but their subsequent ordeal must have been as bad if not worse. In due time the two men were removed from the church by the authorities and in lieu of the gallows they were dressed in sackcloth and made to carry heavy, rough-hewn crosses on a march of some 30 miles to Shoreham for deportation. When they arrived there was no vessel in harbour and the two miscreants were forced to walk into the sea up to their necks every day carrying their crosses until a ship arrived. To have put the crosses down for a second would have meant death.

The Rother rises here, in the cellar of a house called Rotherhurst where a spring bubbles up and begins a 30 mile meandering journey along the Kent border to join the sea at Rye.

The village has a special place in the Sussex Bonfire world. The torchlight processions take place every week over a three month period in towns and villages throughout the county but the season is always launched here at the end of August.

In her memories of childhood in Rotherfield in the 1920s Mrs Dorothy Martin maintained that the children never did anything naughtier than pinch the odd apple. But she did recall that the district nurse, Nurse Ball, kept a parrot for company at her house

149

in Church Road and the local boys managed to teach it to swear one summer by shouting through the open window at the bird. Nurse Ball cottoned on and kept her windows firmly closed after that.

Another feathered friend with a colourful vocabulary was the mynah bird who lived in the bar of The George until his owners moved on in recent years.

Rottingdean ✣

The Americans are a rare breed when it comes to souvenirs. Even so, it must have come as a shock to the parochial church council when the Yanks tried to buy St Margaret's Church in the 1940s. Because of the village's associations with Rudyard Kipling (and the fact that Kipling had an American wife) they wanted to dismantle it, stone by stone, ship it across the Atlantic and re-erect it at the Forest Lawns Cemetery in San Francisco.

Their request was politely refused and so a compromise was reached. The Americans built an exact (from the outside) replica in California and called it the Church of the Recessional, after Kipling's famous poem.

The Rottingdean version of the building is supposed to have been the scene of a grim massacre in 1377 when French pirates landed here. Some of the villagers took shelter in the church tower, and they all perished when the French set fire to it. The tale accounts for the reddish tinges, caused by the extreme heat, which can still be seen on the building today.

The famous have given Rottingdean a veneer of respectability which belies its reputation in the old days as a smuggling hotbed. Sir Edward Burne-Jones, Kipling (who left because the sight-seers got on his nerves), Stanley Baldwin, William Blake, William Watson and William Nicolson ... artists, writers, poets and statesmen all have their links with the village, and it developed something of an 'exclusive' tag as a popular watering hole for convalescents and invalids in the latter years of the last century.

This led to a surge of development (it was the first place in Sussex to have electric light) though something of the jaunty air of a fishing village still remains.

'To be a Rottendeaner you have to be third generation born there'. Or so you will be told by the 'true Rottendeaners', proud that their ancestors were in the village long before it was discovered by the rich and the renowned in Victorian times.

There used to be a saying that Rottingdean donkeys never brayed in daylight. They were too tired after being worked all night by the smugglers, who included Captain Dunk, a butcher who lived at Whipping Post House, and the Rev Thomas Hooker, who acted as lookout man in addition to his role as vicar from 1792 to 1838.

Contraband did not just come in through the village, it went out as well. This smuggling in reverse – illegal exporting rather than importing – was highly lucrative in the 18th century when a Protectionist policy forbade the export of sheep or wool. Those that practised it were called 'owlers', and one Thomas Green was the leader of the successful gang of exponents here.

Sedlescombe

Strange how village history when passed on by word of mouth often contains a vivid phrase that brings the past alive and adds instant authenticity. Ask a Sedlescombe native about the explosion at the gunpowder mills and they will always add the phrase '... and it happened before breakfast.' Four men died in this early morning disaster in December 1764 when the sifting house blew up with a ton of gunpowder inside, including James and Thomas Gilmore, the two sons of the proprietor.

The memory of this hazardous industry lives on in the name of the nearby Powdermill Reservoir. Gunpowder had superseded iron-working, an industry still recalled by the fireback fixed into the wall of the Bridge Garage (once a blacksmith's) which is dated 1649 and depicts Richard Lenard and the tools of his trade. He was the craftsman who fashioned the firebacks before they were moulded.

If you see a plume of smoke rising from the depths of Pettley Woods the chances are it is not a barbecue enthusiast with a fondness for lunch in out-of-the-way locations but men hard at work charcoal burning, a trade which has survived in the area for at least 500 years. There is still a demand for charcoal today for use by industry and today's exponents can trace their roots back to 1424 when the Battle Abbey account books state that the charcoal burners in 'Pettelee Wood' had been paid 6/8d.

An old craft has been given a new lease of life here in more recent times. Farmer Richard Williams opened up a sideline making tiles and bricks at Aldershaw Farm. The little works and kiln cost him £6,000 to set up with a view to turning out about 600 bricks a week using local clay.

The village green has what appears from a distance to be the most picturesque bus shelter in the county. In fact the pillared structure is a well house built in 1900 over the parish pump. It is a handy place on which to record Sedlescombe's triumphs for tidiness: Sussex Rural Community Council plaques show it was the best kept small village in 1985 and in 1979, and the best kept village in all Sussex in 1980. On top of that, it won the county council's anti-litter award in 1981.

The green was the scene of the village Friendly Society's fete every May Day. Perhaps it was on such occasions that the Sedlescombe Ribbon Dance was performed; it would be interesting to know exactly what the 12 dancers did with their ribbons.

The name of the village has become synonymous with the Pestalozzi Children's Village which was established after the Second World War at Oaklands, once the home of the painter Hercules Brabazon. The village, run by a trust, educates poor children from Third World countries. They later return to their homelands to put the skills they have learned here to good use.

A school with less ambitious aims existed in the mid-18th century, a charity establishment to give local children a grounding in the three Rs. In 1755 the elderly master retired and the only man found to replace him was a lad of 18 called Thomas Colbran. He must have been a wise choice for he stayed in charge for 57 years, surely a record for a schoolmaster.

The Victorian writer Coventry Patmore had a liking for Sedlescombe, describing it as surpassing 'all other Sussex villages except Mayfield in its beautiful half-timbered houses of the XVI and XVIIIc. The chief inn of the place is a model of many gabled beauty and bad interior arrangement.'

Hazel trees grow in abundance around here, but make sure

SEDLESCOMBE

you do not go nutting on the sabbath. 'If you go nutting on Sundays the Devil will come to help and hold down the boughs for you.'

Selmeston

The everyday gossip and anecdotes of ordinary folk in this village must have formed the backbone of *A Dictionary of the Sussex Dialect*, the definitive record of the county's peculiarities of speech. It was compiled by the Reverend William Douglas Parish, Vicar of Simpson as it was pronounced in the last century, who captured the words just before the dawn of a more cosmopolitan age when they became obsolete.

Among the fascinating collection of now forgotten words and phrases is a reference to the Sussex belief in fairies or Farisees which endured deep into the 19th century. Parish himself was told and recorded the following yarn in Selmeston:

'I've heard my feather say, that when he lived over the hill, there was a carter that worked on the farm along wid him, and no one couldn't think how t'was that this here man's horses looked so much better than what any one else's did. I've heard my feather say that they was that fat they couldn't scarcely get about; and this here carter he was just as much puzzled as what the rest was, so cardinley he laid hisself up in the staable one night to see if he could find the meaning an't.

'And he hadn't been there very long, before these here liddle farisees they crep in at the sink hole; in they crep, one after another; liddle tiny bits of chaps they was, and each an 'em had a liddle sack of corn on his back as much as ever he could carry. Well: in they crep, on they gets, up they clims, and there they was, just as busy feeding these here horses; and prensley one says to t'other, he says, 'Puck,' says he, 'I twets, do you twet?' And thereupon, this here carter he jumps up and says, 'Dannel ye,' he says, 'I'll make ye twet afore I've done wud ye!' But afore he could get anigh 'em they was all gone, every one an 'em.

'And I've heard my feather say, that from that day forard this here carter's horses fell away, till they got that thin and poor that he couldn't bear to be seen along wid 'em, so he took and went away, for he couldn't abear to see hisself no longer; and nobody aint seen him since.'

The Domesday Book shows that Selmeston was one of the few villages with a priest and it has a rare possession in a 14th century church with wooden pillars, cut with eight sides and with carved capitals. The Rev Parish himself supervised the church's rebuilding in 1866, having each stone marked and reset in its place.

The good vicar was not the sort to have been involved in shadier dealings at the church in the days when the Cuckmere Valley was a hotbed of smuggling. These importers had a rendezvous in the churchyard and an old altar tomb served as a temporary hiding place for their booty. It is said that they never forgot to leave a bottle or two for the parson.

Sheffield Park

Albert Turner hit on an ingenious idea of using water power to run a saw mill on the river Ouse, but it was to prove an expensive flop. He came to Sheffield Park in 1898, probably influenced by the proximity of the railway as a ready-made means of transport for his timber, dug a long mill pond and water channel to the saw mill and must have been delighted to see that all the saws revolved. Unfortunately there was not sufficient power to run all the saws when actually cutting timber and after a few weeks' trial the project was pronounced a failure and a steam engine installed.

Despite the early setback Mr Turner's business flourished and in 1928 his works was reported to be selling first grade ash for 'the building of aeroplanes and certain parts of buses, the residue being used for wheelbarrow legs.' The sawmills is still there today.

Autumn, they say, is the best time to see Sheffield Park Gardens when there are spectacular splashes of colour in the 100 acres of National Trust land originally laid out by 'Capability' Brown and Humphry Repton for the first Earl of Sheffield.

The third Earl was a great cricket fanatic and organised the first tours of Australian cricket teams in England. It was customary for many years for the Aussies to play the first match of the tour at Sheffield Park against Lord Sheffield's XI on a pitch situated near the lakes. Dr W.G. Grace was one of the great names of the day to turn out against the tourists. The last match was played in 1896 but there is a lasting legacy of those days on the other side of the world. The Australian states play for the Sheffield Shield, a trophy presented by the third Earl. By way of variation a match was played on the ice of the frozen lake in the winter of 1881.

The historian Edward Gibbon, writer of *The Decline and Fall of the Roman Empire,* was a friend of the first Earl though a suggestion that he wrote his epic in the library at Sheffield Park is fanciful. It took him a decade to complete, which would suggest a singularly uncommunicative house guest. He died in January 1794 and was buried in the Sheffield Mansoleum at Fletching church.

It was in the 1790s that the Upper Ouse Navigation Trustees were formed to make the inland reaches of the river navigable. Lord Sheffield was chairman and their meetings in the Sheffield Arms appear to have been acrimonious affairs because of the slow progress of the work. The Upper Ouse Navigation had a life

of only 60 years but in that time played its part in creating one of the county's most striking landmarks, the Ouse railway viaduct at Balcombe. Nine million bricks were conveyed up the river by barge.

Lord Sheffield was in the chair again when the Lewes and East Grinstead Railway Company was formed in 1876. The station was at first called Fletching but to comply with the Earl's wishes it soon became Sheffield Park. The station, incidentally, was far more handy for the Sheffield family and their guests than it was for the villagers.

The line closed in the 1950s and was taken over by the Bluebell Railway Preservation Society in 1960 as the first of the preserved steam railways in Britain. Its volunteer staff run vintage locomotives and rolling stock from Sheffield Park to Horsted Keynes five miles away and summer would not be quite the same in this part of the world without the familiar toot of the steam whistle which carries for miles.

If people had to know their place in the old days, and woe betide if you failed to curtsey or bow to Lord Sheffield, there were some fringe benefits. Once a year the work people of the estate were given new boots and red flannel petticoats (the ladies, that is); and as Colonel-in-Chief of the Royal Sussex Regiment, Lord Sheffield welcomed the last of the soldiers to return from the Boer War. They paraded in his grounds and he presented them with a silver cup. Brocks put on a firework display finishing with a grand illumination with the salute: 'Soldiers of Sussex! Best wishes to you all. Sheffield.'

Southease 🦚

Long, dry summers used to create a curious effect on the landscape in these parts. The cement works on the east banks of the Ouse produced (besides cement) a fine, chalky dust which would cake everything in the area. A lengthy spell without any rain to wash it off created something approaching a snowscape. The cement works has now closed.

Gone, too, is a peacock which lived near the railway station and was worth taking a train ride to see. When coaxed and cajoled enough he would fan out his magnificent set of tail feathers for admirers.

The village proper is on the other side of the river across an old iron bridge, now closed to traffic but a good spot for watching some of the water-borne activities such as the annual decorated raft race from Lewes to Newhaven. Southease church is one of only three in the county to have a Norman round tower (see Piddinghoe) and stands majestic in its simplicity beside a miniature village green. Much of it dates back to before the Conquest, given to the abbots of Winchester by King Edgar in 966 AD. Inside there is a much-travelled organ with a mahogany case and gilt pipes built in 1790 by Allen of Soho, which was formerly at St Anne's, Lewes, and then at Offham. There are very few small organs of this date and type in existence and it is in good company. There are others at St Margaret's, Westminster, York Minster and Buckingham Palace.

One of the bells is notable, too. Cast in 1280, it is the third oldest in Sussex.

A widower married again here in 1604, a wedding which must

have been conducted with a fair amount of cynicism by the rector whose entry in minute Latin in the parish records translates as: 'A shipwrecked sailor seeks a second shipwreck.'

South Heighton

Haunting and exorcism in a downland hamlet. It happened in the early years of this century when the tenant of a farmhouse ignored local warnings of a curse on his home by cutting down a line of ancient ilex evergreens which ran down from the church-yard and made his rooms too dark. The deed was done and the curse came true, the farm became haunted with strange sounds as if an invisible presence was forever wandering about the rooms whispering and wailing.

Unable to endure it any longer the tenant and his family left the farm to its ghostly occupant and it was offered rent free for a year to live down the story. But nobody could stand the atmosphere there for more than a few weeks and in addition to the ghostly noises there was now a plaintive, bodiless face gazing with lustr-ous eyes through one of the windows. Finally the vicar, armed with bell, book, candle and incense, performed an exorcism ser-vice in the deserted rooms. There were no further manifestations after that.

South Heighton's heyday was during the life of the cement works which opened in 1885 and before its closure in 1921 employed as many as 150 people.

The church was struck by lightning about 1740. It was never repaired and was condemned for public use in 1780. Gone, too, is The Blacksmith's Arms, the old village hall and the school.

Spithurst

The church echoes on three Sundays a month to the fifth century liturgy of St John Chrystostom spoken in English, Slavonic and occasionally Greek. Because this hamlet in the leafy lane north of Barcombe is the scene of a unique experiment in inter-church co-operation.

Spithurst has one of three Anglican churches in the area administered by the Rev Timothy Fletcher. But as Mr Fletcher uses it only once a month he allows the local Russian Orthodox clergy to use it during the three remaining Sundays. The small congregation of between 15 and 30 people, made up of Russian exiles and converts, is presided over by Arch Priest Serge Hackel, who lives nearby. He described the sharing scheme as a deeply appreciated ecumenical gesture.

Famous for their elaborate ritual, the services have given the church a fresh purpose. Locals still recall the shock in 1969 when plans were announced to close and demolish the building. Large numbers wrote to the local newspaper and 200 signed a petition in protest. The matter went all the way to the judicial committee of the Privy Council, and a year later the Queen signed an order withdrawing the demolition scheme.

Stanmer ℰ

'Telling the bees' is an ancient custom. Bees were notified of all births, marriages and deaths in a family because folk believed that unless this was done the bees would either fly away or die.

Because of the widespread belief of a kinship between men and bees, you can also talk over your problems with the insects. A man living at Stanmer recounted how a drunk once stumbled into his garden and announced: 'I see you have got some bees, I must go and tell them my troubles.' He laid his head on one of the hives and began to talk. Instead of swarming all over the drunk the bees kept absolutely quiet as though listening. Presently the drunk departed, saying 'I feel better now.'

The village and its church are set in a large park, and the 18th century Stanmer Place was once the home of the Pelham family, Earls of Chichester. The village was completely evacuated during the Second World War when it was used as a 'battle school' by the army and suffered much damage. But it was restored to its former glory by Brighton Corporation.

Streat ℘

A tiny place with a big landmark: A massive 'V' on the Downs made from beech, fir and lime trees which was planted in 1887 to mark Queen Victoria's golden jubilee. The 'V' stretches almost from the bottom of the escarpment to the top and is visible for many miles. It makes a nice variation on the chalk carving theme.

Near the Early English church is Streat Place, an Elizabethan beauty built on the site of a much earlier home dating back to before the Conquest and entered in the Domesday Book when the hamlet was Estrat. It was one Walter Dobell who gave the manor house its facade of knapped flints in the classic E plan, as a gesture to Queen Elizabeth. The house stayed in the Dobell family until the middle of the 18th century, during which time it acquired an eerie English Civil War legend. The hall fireplace was said to have a curious hiding place so large that a fugitive Royalist rode his horse inside to escape pursuit and was never seen again.

Also never seen again, in far more recent times, was a £9,000 bronze creation by sculptor John Skelton, who made his home in Streat. The 6ft tall semi-abstract work, weighing 350lbs, was pinched by a muscular thief from the garden. Like so many artists before him, Mr Skelton was left ruefully reflecting that his work was not appreciated. 'It must have been wanted for scrap and that is one of the most hurtful things about it.' he said. 'It would be worth only a few hundred pounds melted down.'

Tarring Neville ℘

Seven cottages, two farms and a church with a total population (at the last count) of 27. Hardly big enough to be classified as a hamlet but a delight for those seeking peace and quiet. It is quite an occasion when a summertime artist sets up an easel here to capture the old buildings and downland beyond.

There used to be many more houses here and the depopulation has been put down to the Black Death, though at the end of the last century there were at least 80 inhabitants.

TARRING NEVILLE

It is the only village in East Sussex with a truly double-barrelled name, thought to be some ancient connection with the Nevill family with lands and property throughout the county. Its relative proximity to the sea must account for the fact that in the church is an iron chest from one of the ships in the Spanish Armada.

Telscombe

The unlovely coastal development sprawls across the cliffs less than a mile away, but in this fold of the Downs is a perfect piece of old England. Untouched and unspoiled.

There is only one way into Telscombe for car travellers and the narrow lane peters out at the end of the village at a spot famous for its bank of wild daffodils in the springtime. A church dating back to Saxon times, a cluster of old cottages and the timeless, empty hills all around ... this remote place is certainly idyllic and owes its character to one man.

Ambrose Gorham, a retired bookmaker, became the squire and benefactor of Telscombe at the end of the last century. He refused to allow any development to take place there but was not a backward-thinking patriarch. He improved the state of the cottages, restored the church of St Lawrence, laid on mains water in 1909 and brought electricity into the village in 1930. Every Christmas he gave each child in his parish a book and a pair of Wellington boots.

Squire Gorham never lost his taste for the sport of kings and trained many winners at his Telscombe stables. The most famous product of the Downland 'Gallops' was *Shannon Lass,* winner of the Grand National in 1902.

When he died in 1933, the squire bequeathed all his land to Brighton Corporation on trust, stating in his will that the purpose of the gift was to preserve the rural nature of the village. Significantly, as an ex-bookie, he stipulated that the incumbent should be non-teetotal and should be a smoker. The Gorham Trust exists to this day, ensuring that the village retains its tranquility.

In earlier days, Telscombe man James Lulham gained an unfortunate place in the record books as the last man in England to be hanged for sheep stealing. He went to the gallows in 1819.

Ticehurst

Public servants are scarcely as loyal or as versatile as old William Harris, who at the age of 85 was persuaded 'by several friends' to print a card for distribution among his fellow parishioners in January, 1876, listing his achievements in local public life.

William stated that he had lived in Ticehurst for 73 years during which time he had been 'van and fly operator 53 years; collector of taxes 46 years; Post Office 30 years; High Constable 46 years; one of the principals of the Church Choir 25 years; Surveyor of Highways to the general satisfaction of the Parish (so it is recorded in the Vestry Book) 28 years; Tenant to Church Gate Estate 38 years.'

An earlier Ticehurst worthy was less diverse, but his parish duty was just as important: John Rodgers was solemnly appointed 'Dog Whiper in the Church' at a vestry meeting in 1710 at a salary of two shillings a quarter. It was also decided 'that if any boyes made a noyes he complains of them to there parents the first time.' Presumably a second offence allowed Mr Rodgers to double the role of 'Dog Whiper' with 'Boye Whiper'. The church's 'Doom' window, where the 14th century stained glass shows the fate of sinners being carted off to purgatory by demons, should have been enough to put thoughts of mischief out of young minds.

Naughty boys who failed to mend their ways in manhood might have found themselves confined in the village lock-up, a chamber above the church porch, or in the 'parish cage' which seems to have occupied various sites including a corner of the churchyard in the 1850s.

The true felon would have had the Ticehurst Prosecuting Society to contend with. Before the establishment of an efficient county police force the inhabitants depended on voluntary efforts to bring offenders to justice. This society was formed to raise a fund for prosecuting villains and to pay rewards to anyone offering information that led to their conviction. 200 years ago the reward payable on the conviction of a horse thief (£10) was the same as that offered for the conviction of a murderer.

The agricultural riots of 1830 brought a mob 400 strong to Ticehurst where they roughed up the master of the poor house in the early hours, went quiet as lambs past the home of 90-year-old Mrs Newington so as not to disturb her slumbers, and proceeded to Pashley intent on destroying a threshing machine that was used there. It was locked away in the coach house and when Major Richard Wetherell appeared in his militia uniform armed with a sword and pistol threatening to shoot the first man who entered the building the rioters dispersed.

If life for the agricultural labourers was hard at this time, it was even harder for parish paupers, who were not even allowed to drown their sorrows. The village publicans were warned that their licences would not be renewed if they did not call time at 10pm as many paupers had been seen past that time 'drinking, and oftentime to excess' to the great expense of 'all persons paying taxes.' There was to be no gambling, and travellers were the only people to be served during Divine Service on the sabbath.

Whether the serenity of this High Weald village is conducive to a long life only today's residents can tell. The Rev A. Kesteman certainly thought so in 1794 when he waxed lyrical about the advantages enjoyed by his flock in terms of respectability, sociability and charitability. 'The inhabitants herabouts live to a good old age and many exceed the common limits of life very far indeed.'

In the following century the *Sussex Express* thought it was worth noting that Ticehurst glover John Edwards, aged 94, walked from the village to Lewes, a distance of 24 miles, 'without any inconvenience to himself. Notwithstanding his vast age, Mr Edwards can still make a glove with neatness and dispatch.'

September was a boom time in the village in this century when London's East Enders came to pick hops on their annual holiday. The shops used to extend their hours of business because the hop-pickers were renowned as cheerful spenders.

Ticehurst was the home for some years of Thomas Blinks (1860-1912) the artist who specialised in sporting life pictures, and, for the record, the first high explosive bombs on England in the Second World War dropped here on May 22nd, 1940.

Udimore

Did the angels give this sparse place its name? Legend says the church was originally planned for a different site in the marshes of Brede Level but that no progress was made on the building because every night the stones had been mysteriously moved to a new location. The villagers stayed up to watch what was going on and through the darkness saw a host of angels carrying away the building materials while the breeze carried their chant: 'O'er the mere! O'er the mere!'

The church was completed on the more suitable site the heavenly bodies had selected and the village around it became O'er there mere – Udimore. Less glamorous is eau de mer, from the fact that the sea once came much closer than it does today, and less glamorous still is 'Boundary of the Wood', from the *Oxford English Dictionary of Place Names*.

By an ancient edict church fonts were not to be made of wood and the churchwardens here in the 18th century were either too poor or too mean to buy a new one. So they carried out an ingenious forgery on Udimore's strange little pudding bowl font, carefully painting the outside of the wooden bowl like weathered stone and the inside like lead.

There are several testaments to the fact that the inhabitants of the village can expect a long life (maybe it is something to do with the eau de mer) and a tablet in the church records: 'Death will come at last. To the memory of Widow Marshall, late of this parish, who died the 9th day of March 1798. Aged 98 years. Erected by Benj. Cooper, gent. of this parish.' Poor Ben, though, followed the good widow into the grave at the age of only 38!

Edwards I and III stayed at Court Lodge, and while the latter was busy building Winchelsea his Queen stood on the Udimore ridge and watched a sea fight with the Spaniards.

A far more recent conflict earned a slice of glory for village shopkeeper Eric Field. *The Sussex Express* reported during the Second World War that when a Messerschmitt fighter was shot down here the gallant Mr Field took the German pilot prisoner and locked him up in his shop until the army arrived.

Two Udimore families were famous as members of a gang of smugglers based at The Red Lion in Brede. It took a big chunk out of the tiny population when menfolk from the Whiteman and Millis families were indicted at Horsham Assizes in 1828 and sentenced to transportation.

A look at the map will help you understand the answer when a Sussex person asks you where the flies go in the winter – 'through Udimore to Brede, of course.'

Wadhurst

The last important bare-fisted prize fight in England took place here on December 8, 1863. The combatants were Tom King, an Englishman, and a giant American called Heenan, who had been known to wrestle and even attempt to throttle his opponents.

King was a stone lighter than Heenan's 15st 7lbs, but youth and ability were on his side in a fight lasting a punishing 36 rounds and the Englishman eventually won the day.

A special party of spectators had left London Bridge at 6.15am in a special train of 30 carriages, which 'drew up at a secluded spot short of Wadhurst station at 9.15am,' according to the *pugilistica* reporter. The party then 'toiled up a steep clayey hill for about 1½ miles' to the venue of the contest at Sparrows Green.

The brutality of the fight caused a public outcry and calls for reform. As a result public prize-fighting was made illegal. Another upset party was the tenant of the land where the fight stakes were pitched. Old John Wallis came back from his holidays to find his meadow damaged, and his hedges and gates broken by the crowd.

Churchwardens in the old days had some strange duties. The Wadhurst accounts show that the parish was expected to pay for the control of vermin and the churchwarden was expected to dole out the cash (and join in). An extract from 1656-8 reads:

	s.	d.
1656. Paid to Mr Barham of Butts for 3 dozen of bullfinches	3	6
To him more for Jayes	1	0
And for Crowes, Rooks and Hedge Hogs	1	0
Paid myself more for 72 Bullfinches	6	0
Allowed to Longley for killing Badger	1	0
1658. Allowed for vermins' Heads	19	4

The ruthless decimation of bullfinches is a puzzle, as is another local custom of hunting for squirrels on Good Friday.

It was the iron industry that laid the foundation for Wadhurst's wealth as testified by the church's collection of 30 iron floor slabs, the most in the county, and by the many fine houses in this mellow village.

Old habits die hard it seems. The iron industry had disappeared north to the coalfields at least a century before an attempt was made to revive it here in August 1857 after the arrival of the railway. Sussex ore was mined in Snape Wood and then transported by train to Staffordshire for smelting. It proved impractical and was abandoned in September 1858.

Oak trees, 'The Sussex Weed', fed the furnaces and also went from Whiligh in the parish to repair the roof of the Great Hall at Westminster in 1922 and 1948, the Courthope family sending the best from their estate. It was one George Courthope who nearly three centuries earlier was knighted by Charles II, an honour slightly tarnished when he later sent a bill for £72 as 'expenses' for the knighthood.

As early as 1253 Wadhurst was granted a charter to hold a May fair on the feast of St Peter and St Paul, and it was still going strong when Mayfield schoolmaster Walter Gale noted in his diary on May 29th, 1750: 'I went to the fair at Wadhurst. Took a turn in the fair where on sweethearts and maidenheads I laid out 2d.'

The charter also included a weekly market, which survived in the village as a livestock market until August 1982. The name lives on at Heathfield, however, where the Wadhurst Fat Stock Show is a popular feature.

A November day in 1956 is still recalled with sadness here. An RAF Meteor jet, being flown low over the village by a local young man, crashed into The Queen's Head in the High Street, completely demolishing the ancient coaching inn, the nearby stores and a bungalow. The pilot, his navigator and four civilians were all killed.

Maurice Tate, the Sussex and England cricketer, became landlord at The Greyhound after his retirement from the game. He must have felt at home in a village where cricket has always had a strong following and been played since the 18th century. But football was here first; 13 Wadhurst men were fined for playing it in 1548 when the amusements of the poorer classes were at that time severely repressed as part of a general policy adopted by the young King Edward VI.

One man who knows more than most about the village's more recent past is Charlie Bocking, who was born in 1898 and built-up a huge collection of old photographs, documents and newspaper cuttings concerning Wadhurst which he has presented to the parish. Charlie, grandson of the village schoolmaster who served from 1851 to 1890, lost many of his old school friends during the First World War. No fewer than 24 Wadhurst men, from the Royal Sussex Regiment, were killed on a single day at Festubert in May 1915.

Waldron ✒

After a drink or two at the old Star Inn the senses can start to play strange tricks. What was that eerie sound coming from over the way in the churchyard? The locals put down their glasses to listen and a hush fell upon the bar. There it was again ... a ghostly groaning? A malignant icy whisper? The sound of a damned soul in torment?

Emboldened by the ale, some of the younger men in the assembled throng left the genial glow of the pub and stepped out into the wintry night to investigate the mystery. The church was outlined starkly against the moonlight and the chilling noise grew louder as they picked their way cautiously through the graveyard. It seemed to be coming from the tower itself ... then there was a sudden squawk of alarm, a furious flapping of wings and an owl abandoned its slumbering place in the belfry where its sonorous snoring had been magnified dramatically by the enclosed space.

The Waldron ghost hunt found its way into the pages of the *Sussex Express* a few years back. A newspaper from an earlier age carried a more inexplicable story in 1756: 'On Monday January 19 between 9 and 10am a great noise like thunder was heard in a well belonging to the Rev Hamlin at Waldron. On examination the water was found to be several feet higher than usual and in great ferment and agitation which subsided in about 15 minutes. Between 10 and 11 it returned and continued for half-an-hour which greatly alarmed the neighbourhood.'

Things grow well around this picturesque and compact village. Just below the church, is a lane turned almost into a leafy tunnel with rocks on either side, are St George's Vineyards, where the English wine has rapidly made a name for itself – as far afield as Japan, in fact, with big orders from Tokyo. And Bentham and Hooker's British Flora asserts that the Spiked Rampion (*Phyteuma spicatum*) is found only about Waldron.

The village pond used to be beside the church and was used by the forge until it was filled in during the 1930s. It is spring fed and has bubbled to the surface again in the past. Now tarmaced over, there are still a few villagers who keep a close eye on things, half-hoping to see this relic of the past force its way back into life again.

In the church tower is a peal of eight bells, with certificates to mark the excellence of the Waldron bellringers. One, dated March 1890, states that 'eight parishioners rang on the bells in this tower a full and complete Grandsire triples (5,040) changes.' They achieved this feat in three hours and one minute.

Just outside the church door is one of the three great Saxon fonts in Sussex, a round monster hewn from a single block of stone. It had been lost for years and the story goes that it was found on a farm where it served as a cattle trough. Another yarn elaborates: that it was taken out of the church by Cromwell's men and rolled down the hill.

This is a secretive village buried away in a maze of lanes and pointed at, but never quite pinpointed, by a score of signposts. Yet the parish has produced two Lord Mayors of London, the first being Sir William de Walderne in 1412 and the second Sir Thomas Offley of Possingworth in 1657, who left half his estate to the poor and was a man so abstemious in his habits that he inspired the rhyme:

'Offley three dishes had of daily roast –
An egg, an apple, and the third of toast.'

Food on a grander scale than the diet of good Sir Thomas is the subject of The Waldron Cauldron, a book of recipes contributed by parishioners and compiled by Thelma Stevens, Iris Newson and the Rev David Paskins. It includes several traditional Sussex recipes, including Lardy Johns:

4 oz lard	4 oz flour
1½ tsp baking powder	4 oz sugar
½ oz currants	

Method: Rub the lard into the flour, then add baking powder. Add currants. Mix into a stiff paste with water, roll out into two-inch squares and bake for 10–15 minutes.

Or how about a cure for night cramps, a prescription given by Sir

Morton Smart, Physician to King George VI:

> At bedtime, add to a tumbler of hot water two round tsps of glucose, ½ tsp bicarb of soda and 2 tsps of lemon juice. Drink every night before retiring until cramp is cured.

Wannock

A formidable lady believed to be more than 300 years old is still going strong today. She used to reside at Wannock's ancient watermill, powered by one of several streams rising in the chalk hills above the village, but since the mill's demolition has moved to more suburban surroundings.

The lady in question is a wooden carving, which used to stand at the front of the building. In his book *The Road and the Inn*, written in 1917, Hissey gave an account of his meeting with the strange likeness: 'My attention was arrested by a badly carved and brightly coloured figure of a woman ... shown holding a bowl grasped in one hand, and in the other an upraised long rolling pin.' He was told by the miller that the figure was thought to be 300 years old and depicted an earlier miller's wife.

And the bowl and rolling pin? When the gleaners brought their corn she took a 'toll' of a gallon bowl of grain, levelling it off with the pin, and ground the rest free of charge.

A few years ago the figure disappeared, but was spotted in a Brighton antiques shop and bought by the Turner family of Polegate who have it in safe keeping – fitting custodians as the family used to run the Mill House Bakery in Wannock.

In 1827 James Seymour became tenant miller and farmer. His two sons Joseph and Stephen moved into a more lucrative field of business with the local smuggling fraternity. Joseph would make two or three trips to France each year to arrange the purchase of contraband which was then carried over in French boats and landed at Birling Gap and Cow Gap, and from there to secure hiding places. There are still secret passages at Wannock Place and the Old Mill House.

Joseph ploughed his proceeds from this profitable sideline

into more legitimate activities, building a windmill at Polegate, a new watermill at Wannock and establishing the extensive strawberry field in the village's Walnut Street. It was Joseph's great-grandson Charles Thomas who branched out from strawberry cultivation in 1895 to open 'Charlie's Tea Gardens'. There was local bread, a strawberry tea of course, and a special little loaf was provided for each child who paid a visit. The venture flourished until the outbreak of the Second World War.

The area was a base for airships during the First World War, patrolling the coastal waters for U Boats and also carrying out 'spotting' work for the artillery in France. There was a tragedy just before Christmas in 1917 when one of the airships lost its way in fog and darkness. It landed on the Aldis lamp of another airship moored on the Downs, the envelope split and the exhaust ignited the escaping hydrogen. The pilot died in the flames and two crew members were badly burned. The moored airship also caught fire and Lieutenant Victor Watson bravely rushed into the inferno to make sure all the crew had escaped. He lost his right arm when two 65lb bombs on board exploded. Iron mooring rings, set in concrete on the hills, are the only relic today of the base.

Warbleton

The War-bil-in-Tun is the name of the pub. Is it an appalling pun on the name of the village or, as the story goes, a name provided by an historical event? They say an impatient solider came this way centuries ago and in his greed for beer when he arrived at the ale house chopped open the barrel with his bill or halberd. Get it?

In the tower of the church opposite was imprisoned Richard Woodman, most famouse of the Sussex martyrs. Woodman was a local ironmaster who in the middle of the 16th century publicly accused the curate of being a religious turncoat, changing from Protestant to Catholic to suit the monarch of the day. Woodman, whose business yielded £900 a year and who had 100 men on his payroll, paid dearly for his outspoken views. He was forced to become a fugitive from the law, hiding in a wood for six weeks where his devoted wife brought him food, and later escaping to

Flanders. He returned after less than a month and hid in his own house, eluding arrest until he was betrayed and finally burnt on a grid iron at Lewes in 1557 with other Protestant martyrs of the Maryan persecution.

Warbleton has always had a strong dissenting element. A century after Woodman's death the churchwardens complained that there were 19 Quakers, six Anabaptists and nine other parishioners who did not attend church. Christian's River got its name because it was ideal for full immersion baptisms.

Warbleton is the name of the parish, but the true village settlement is Rushlake Green, a mile or so to the east with its pretty circle of cottages around a green. The green is not particularly big and led to the village cricket club introducing its own variation of the game. Boundary scores were not adopted until 1903, with three runs for a shot which bounced off the green, four runs for a shot that cleared it without bouncing and six runs for the mighty batsman who could clout the ball clear over the circle of houses.

Despite the eccentricity of scoring, the club seems to have taken the game seriously enough and in the early years of this century complained about the Warbleton Friendly Society, whose merry-making on the green was damaging the pitch. In 1905 the parish council approved that part of the green should be enclosed to protect the wicket.

The Friendly Society was founded in 1855 with members paying a certain amount every year in return for compensation for sickness, medical attention and funerals. With the money left over the society had a feast day at Rushlake Green on the second Tuesday in May. Members were given a slap-up dinner at The Horse and Groom which included roast beef and Christmas pudding. By 1896 the society had its own uniformed band and the feast days grew more lavish with roundabouts and sideshows on the green which so upset the cricketers.

The Misses Darby brought a little joy to Warbleton during the dark days of the First World War. At Christmas in 1915 they treated 60 schoolchildren to an entertainment featuring Professor Bontolf, 'Wizard of the South', and Ada Lill, 'the girl illusionist.' All the children left at the end of the day with a toy 'mysteriously produced from fairyland.'

The war brought to an end the parish's main industry – chicken fattening. Higglers, dealers in chicken, would buy up chicks which were crammed (forcibly fed on a machine) and then taken off to market. Many of the breeding stock were killed in the food panic which came with the war.

There was also a living to be made in bricks, with brickworks at Three Cups, Turners Green and Foords Farm. Hops, too, were grown extensively in the area and nearly every farm possessed an oast house. The fact that the Warbleton woods are rich in chestnut trees is a remnant of those days when they were deliberately planted because the timber was popular for hop poles.

But there was always poverty. Warbleton parish officers had in 1825 bought property to house the many paupers of the parish including three hovels at Bodle Street which went by the unlovely name of Mud Castle. Ten years later the poor house opposite the church had 19 people crowded in it. Eight of them were over 70 and two were illegitimate boys of nine.

John Blackman, who owned several farms in the area, had his own way of bringing a little comfort to the poor. Before he died in 1854 he directed that eight of his old labourers should carry his coffin at his funeral for which they were to be paid £1 each.

Man's brief span is the subject of an inscription found on a pane of glass in recent years at Pleydells, Rushlake Green. Dated 1763, it reads: 'Abraham Holman is my name, and England is my nation; Rushlake Green was my Dwelling Place, but not long Habitation.'

Lonely Warbleton Priory, dating from the days of Henry IV and in later years a farm, hotel and restaurant, has a rather sinister reputation. Bloodstains leave an indelible mark on the floor of one of the rooms there, and two skulls are preserved in the building. When any attempt was made to bury them there were terrible noises in the night and it was believed that the cattle on the locals farms fell sick.

Wartling

Stories travel round villages at great speed and they sometimes get twisted in the telling. The Legend of the Black Rat caused some alarm in Wartling with grim rumours that the deadly plague had returned to the village 300 years after it claimed so many victims here.

Mr Kemeys Bagnall-Oakeley had to allay the fears and set the record straight with the full story in the parish magazine. He had set about modernising his home, School House Farm, and had taken down the ceilings to expose the old beams. The spaces in between were packed with reeds and when they were brought tumbling to the floor he discovered they harboured the mummified corpses of black rats – the kind that were indeed responsible for spreading the plague. He had one of the bodies examined at the Natural History Museum in London and it was established that the rodent dated from around 1669 – when the disease hit Wartling.

Unfortunately, the word got round that Mr Bagnall-Oakeley had discovered a live black rat ... hence his piece in the parish magazine.

German prisoners of war were set to work laying piped water to this pretty village on the edge of the billiard table green of Pevensey Levels. At least, they wore German army uniforms and it was not until after the war that villagers discovered the men who had done them a good turn (albeit under duress) were in fact Russians, captured by the Germans and given the option of remaining prisoners or serving the Fatherland as non-combatants. They had been taken prisoner a second time, by the British, at St Valery.

Unfortunately they had a German sense of measurement and seem to have confused the depth of the trench for the main between 30 inches and 30 millimetres. As a result the mains are so shallow that periodically a lorry fractures one and Wartling has to put up with brown water until it is repaired.

In the old days when their wells ran dry the villagers had to travel to the wind pump in Hooe Lane which drew water. It lay at the bottom of a steep hill known in the days before Tarmac as Jacob's Ladder because the steady plod of the cows had built the slope into a long series of ridges. The remains of the wind pump are still there today.

There are two heronries in Wartling, one of them established in a series of fir trees at Coopers Farm which retired farmworker

Bert Honeysett can remember planting. They underwent a strange transformation during the severe winter of 1963 which caused them to branch out horizontally because of the weight of the snow. The herons find this zig-zag effect in the branches ideal.

It is fitting that the lectern at the church should be in the shape of a heron, not the standard eagle, a magnificent specimen with a five foot wingspan carved in wood. It attracts more comments in the visitors' book than any other feature, though it does cause some confusion. Somebody said how much they liked the church's swan, and another said how appropriate it was, when baptisms were being performed in the church, to have a stork on hand.

West Dean

The Lamplands and the Taperlands have long disappeared from this delightful conservation village, tucked away in a corner of Friston Forest. They were fields, the rents from which went to the church to pay for oil to keep a lamp burning above the altar, and to buy tapers or candles for the building.

At West Dean can be found what is maintained to be the oldest inhabited rectory in the country, dating in part from 1220 with flint and stone walls two and a half feet thick and a stone spiral staircase. With such an old timer about it is possible to believe that Alfred the Great had his palace here. Certainly Asser, the monk who was to become a bishop and the King's biographer, was summoned to visit Alfred and recorded his royal welcome at West Dean.

Charleston Manor, a little to the north and looking out across the River Cuckmere, was bought by the artist Sir Oswald Birley in 1931 and he commissioned architect Walter Godfrey to restore the Norman building. The barn alongside the house became the portrait painter's studio and doubled as a small theatre with a stage for actors and musicians. It became the venue for the annual Charleston Festival.

When the Rev G.W. A. Lawrance was appointed rector at West Dean in 1891 he led the excavation of the lost village of Exceat, which had been incorporated with West Dean in 1528. A stone marks the site of their investigation. Exceat was quite an important fishing community with 24 taxpayers in 1296, but a mighty storm destroyed the anchorage used by the fishing fleet and then the Black Death and raids by the French finished the village as a community.

There used to be a cottage here haunted by a number of ghosts who all shared the same background – they had been driving or riding on carts climbing the hill from the river valley and been killed when they tumbled off on the sharp gradient.

Westfield

Dark deeds and a mystery on Bonfire Night. Westfield's last windmill went up in flames on November 5, 1908, on the evening when the village's bonfire society was making its annual torchlight procession around the large houses of the village.

The finger of suspicion pointed naturally enough to the Bonfire Boys and they were openly accused of causing the destruction. But they pleaded their innocence and in time people came to the conclusion that they had not been guilty after all of the illegal addition to the pyrotechnic display. The true culprit was never discovered.

The bonfire society has gone, so too have the point-to-point meetings at Church Place Farm and Wheel Farm. The annual beating of the bounds is no longer practised, although some of the Westfield boundary stones are still there. Waiting perhaps for a return of the days when once again the choirboys will be bumped on them to impress on their young minds the limits of their parish. Choirboys were not the only victims of the tradition. There is a photograph of burly village blacksmith William Eaton being bumped by his Edwardian contemporaries which forms part of a pictorial record of old Westfield compiled and exhibited by Ruth Clements and her husband Don.

It shows the tremendous growth that has taken place in the past two decades, though the village is still far enough removed from Hastings to retain its own identity. Expansion is nothing new; the church, which has an oak door dated 1542, dates from

Saxon times and had to be extended in 1251 to accommodate the growing numbers of the faithful.

Westham 🌿

The village lies, literally, in the shadow of Pevensey Castle, but Westham has its own identity and is anxious to preserve it. When it was proposed to combine the village with Pevensey to make one parish named Anderida the message from the packed public meeting was a firm 'Hands off.'

The church was built soon after the Normans landed and in the churchyard lie the 'plague stones', four unmarked stones in the shape of a cross which mark the communal grave of the victims of the disastrous epidemic of 1666. An old sexton was said to have been scared to dig a new grave near them, and local tradition says that there was a pest house nearby.

A shameless piece of ecclesiastical vandalism was carried out by the Rev Howard Hopley in 1860 when he took part in the excavations of the first temple of Jerusalem. He chipped off a splinter of stone which was set in onyx and marble, and fixed it to the wall of the church during Hopley's incumbency from 1885 to 1917 with the legend: 'Fragment of Solomon's Temple.'

Another vicar of Westham tried (in vain) to keep Charles II on the straight and narrow path of morality. Brian Duppa, vicar here in 1625, was made Dean of Christ Church and Chancellor of Oxford, then consecrated Bishop of Chichester, translated to Salisbury and finally to Winchester in 1660. He was tutor to Charles II, having spent much time with his ill-fated father. The Merry Monarch seems to have had a real affection for the holy man, and also some feelings of remorse for not having adhered to his spiritual guideline. The King repeatedly visited the Bishop as he lay on his deathbed, knelt at his side and craved his blessing.

Another Westham clergyman of note was William Leeke, curate from 1829, who was a standard bearer at the Battle of Waterloo. He held special services for coastguards stationed in the Martello towers in these parts. They were held at irregular hours so the smugglers would not know when no watch was being kept.

Westmeston ❦

The census of 1871 shows that there were 40 houses in Westmeston, 136 men and boys, 107 women and girls. The Downland hamlet is not much bigger today, but it has certainly got more than its fair share of ghosts.

Black Dog Hill takes its name from a particularly unnerving phantom, a headless black dog which roams the area howling. It was supposedly chasing game when spotted by a gamekeeper who let fly with his blunderbuss and shot the unfortunate animal's head off. Then there is the ghostly monk who carves at a panel in Westmeston Place, waking up the occupants of the bedroom, or the nun that serenely walks from the church of St Martin, through the north wall of Church Cottage and across the road. On a grander scale there is the phantom army on the Downs, where the sound of horses' hoofs and the moans of men can be heard, accompanied by a particularly nasty smell, on May 24th, 25th and 26th. Did the men flee from the Battle of Lewes? No-one in the village can be sure, but many have testified to that peculiar odour.

Westmeston was the home of the heavenly twins, Jack Vigar and Harry Piper. They were sent home early from the village school in 1881 because of a tremendous snowstorm. Their way led over the hill but the blizzard blocked out all light and the seven-year-olds, stumbling and exhausted, became completely lost. Then a mysterious shepherd took them by the hands, told them they were on the Dyke and going in the wrong direction. He guided them safely home. Who he was or where he came from they never discovered, but if it was Divine Guidance then Jack and Harry lived up to their early experience 'growing to be fine men who were never known to tell a lie.' For the rest of their lives they were called the 'heavenly twins'.

Whatlington ❦

Weatherboard cottages and a much-restored church on the road east of Battle where some residents are prepared to take major steps to maintain the serenity of the place. Villagers went to the courts in 1984 to try and stop motorcycle scramble racing in the village.

Noise levels were measured and the Grass Enduro Scramble Trial (Off Road) Motorcyle Club peaked at 72 decibels during one of their Sunday meetings in Whatlington (120 decibels is the pain threshold to the human ear). The noise was described as 'appalling' by the complainants, but a petition signed by other residents saying they did not object to the races was produced and magistrates upheld an appeal against a ban on racing on condition there were only two meetings a year, between 10am and 4pm.

The mind boggles as to what a one-time Lord of the Manor of Whatlington would have made of all this. He was no less a figure than King Harold who held the manor until 1066 and in later years it was owned by the Pelhams and Ashburnhams. John De Watlyngton was made Abbot of Battle in 1307.

There are two mysteriously named woods within half a mile of each other in this parish. But why one is called Maddomswood and the other Maddoms Wood, no one knows.

Wilmington

The Long Man of Wilmington towers above the village on Windover Hill. This faceless outline of a man carved into the chalk, standing 227ft high with two staves in his hands slightly longer than himself, still remains a mystery. Was he created by the monks at the priory? Is he of Roman origin? Or do his roots lie in the Neolithic period?

There are many theories about his identity, from a giant killed on this spot by a hammer thrown by another who lived at Firle to an ancient god throwing open the gates of dawn, but the Long Man is giving nothing away as he faces sightless but serene across the Weald. Unlike the Cerne Giant in Dorset he is sexless, and this has prompted enthusiastic attempts to remedy the situation. The offending additions to his anatomy have been hastily removed.

Wilmington has lost its baker, butcher, blacksmith and general store. Even the village pond where the carters used to water their horses has been filled in and the cottages of the farmworkers and craftsmen have a new breed of occupants. But if the days of self-sufficiency have gone there have been compensations. The old buildings have been lovingly restored to form one of the most picturesque village streets in the county.

The priory was established in the 13th century with additions in the 14th and 15th centuries. It was an 'alien' house, belonging to the Abbey of Grestain in Normandy, and therefore suspect, and it was frequently seized during the wars with the French. It was suppressed in 1414 in common with all the other alien houses and eventually fell into ruin. The priory was acquired by the Sussex Archaeological Trust and now forms an attractive feature at the end of the single street.

It stands beside the church which boasts one of the oldest yew trees in the county. It was growing before the arrival of the Conqueror and its 23ft girth is now supported by posts and chains. The strange 'Wilmington Madonna' in the chancel was removed from an exterior wall and its rather gargoyle-like appearance has led to the suggestion that it could have pre-Christian origins as a pagan fertility symbol.

The old Sussex family of Ade have had strong connections with Wilmington down the centuries as their many resting places in the churchyard testify. Mr Peter Ade owned the site of the 'tin chapel' of the Congregationalists, now demolished, where the district council built the Ade's Field estate.

Between the wars Wilmington would ring to the band music of the Territorials, who camped on the Downs, and other visitors were the gipsies (Didicais to the locals, a name of respect meaning gipsies of the better sort, not like Mumpers or Pikers). They used to camp on the green while they helped the farmers through the summer's heavy workload.

The artist Harold Swanick and his wife lived in the village for many years, mistletoe growing in the apple trees of their garden at Street Farm. Hollywood star Ronald Colman was a frequent guest of the Swanicks and the actor Percy Marmont lived in Wilmington before the Second World War.

Several ghosts have also favoured this place. There was a peg-legged sailor who sat in a chair in the village street smoking a clay pipe, and the eerie light which haunted one of the cottages and led the beholder into outbuildings before disappearing. The residents of The Chantry were so alarmed when they saw the spirit of an old lady gliding down the garden path that they slammed the door and locked it. There was a strange twist. They made inquiries and established tha the apparition they had seen, which was certainly not tangible, was of somebody who was still alive. A living ghost, if that is not a contradiction in terms.

The Chantry, which has a stone face above the front door said to be a caricature of one of the village's clergymen carved by sculptor with a sense of humour or an axe to grind, was once a school. It was run by an elderly woman who had a tough approach to young offenders. They were tied to a beam with a cord and threatened with a visit from the blacksmith to pull out their teeth with his tongs.

Winchelsea

John Wesley, the great apostle of the 18th century, preached his last open air sermon here under a great ash tree on October 7th, 1790. He noted in his journal: 'It seemed as if all that heard were, at the present, almost persuaded to be Christians.'

If his views about the future piety of the inhabitants were uncertain, he had very definite ideas about the nature of the place itself. 'That poor skeleton of ancient Winchelsea,' he called it. 'It is beautifully situated on the top of a steep hill, and was regularly built in broad streets, crossing each other and encompassing a very large square, in the midst of which was a large church, now in ruins.'

While most towns are villages that grew, this place did the reverse with a history that has been singularly unlucky. It had its own mint before the conquest and by the 11th century was a port of considerable importance. But in 1250 it was partially submerged by the sea, and matters were not helped 16 years later when Prince Edward sacked the place to put an end to the indiscriminate piracy that was rife among Winchelsea's seamen. Another great storm destroyed the old settlement in 1287.

A fresh start was made on a new site with a model new town

which must have been the medieval planner's dream and was designed on the grid system. With its tidal harbour on the river Brede, Winchelsea became a member of the Cinque Ports Confederation, providing ships for the country's defence. But repeated raids by the French devastated the place with great slaughter and the Deadman's Lane of today marks the area where the victims were buried. Finally the sea retreated, the harbour silted up and the once proud port was marooned.

There was a revival of fortunes during the 16th and 17th centuries when refugees from France brought their weaving skills, but by the end of the 18th century the once great fair on May 14 had dwindled to a shabby version of pedlars and gingerbread.

Wesley's ash tree was uprooted in 1927 but another has replaced it. There is an old photograph, taken in 1867, of an old lady of 84 called Asenath Jones. When Wesley came to Winchelsea he was the guest of her father, and he is pictured beside the chair on which the preacher had sat with the young Asenath on his knee.

Two Members of Parliament were returned until the Reform Act of 1832 when the last pair of MPs, James Brougham and Judge Williams, voted for the abolition of the 'rotten borough' they themselves represented. Later a Royal Commission recommended the abolition of the mayor and corporation, but though Winchelsea lost its magisterial and other functions the corporation was allowed to remain in existence to administer a sum of less than £20 a year derived from town rents and royal dues. Every Easter Monday a mayor and other corporate officials continue to be elected with due pomp and ceremony for this purpose at a Hundred Court in the ancient Court Hall.

Lace was made here a century or so ago, mainly by small children apprenticed by Overseers of the Poor in neighbouring parishes, and in the late 19th century Mrs Skinner of Periteau House launched a lace making school.

Two distinguished men of law came from Winchelsea. Henry Peter Brougham MP and Thomas Denman gained royal gratitude (and displeasure from the other party) when they successfully defended Queen Caroline against the attempt to dissolve her marriage to King George IV in 1820.

The actress Dame Ellen Terry lived at Tower Cottage for a

WINCHELSEA

number of years. The 'painters' actress' was immortalised by some of the great artists of the Victorian and Edwardian age. She never sat for Millais despite the fact that at one time they were neighbours here. Dame Ellen gave great encouragement to the parish's own amateur theatricals, and is remembered for her kindness by the locals. At the turn of the century every child's shoe in Winchelsea was said to have been supplied by her.

Visitors to the Castle Inn see ties before their eyes in the saloon bar – and that is before they have had a drink! The ties, more than 50 of them at the last count in all colours and sizes, have been handed in by retired colonels, majors and generals who are regulars at the pub. When landlord Derrick Baldock and his wife Lena took over they discovered there were quite a few military men in the area and the idea of collecting their regimental ties just snowballed.

Withyham

'The village by the water where the willow trees grow.' A lyrical name for a lovely place, described by the writer E.V. Lucas as the Jewel of Sussex.

Farmer Edward Frisby Howis certainly loved the place so much that he stated in his will that he should have a spy hole in his grave to look out across his acres at Sunnyford Farm. Accordingly when he was buried in Withyham churchyard in the early years of the last century a length of drainpipe was designed to run from his grave to an outlet with a view of the open countryside.

The steep climb to the church, with its view across a lake to Hartfield's spire piercing the distant woodland, is worth getting out of breath for. The building contains many memorials to the Sackville and de la Warr families, the most impressive being Caius Cibber's sculptured monument to Thomas Sackville, who died in 1677 at the age of 13. The life size marble figures of his parents, in contemporary dress, kneel on cushions gazing sadly at the boy, who reclines holding a skull (to signify death in infancy). Around the table tomb is a frieze of children.

It is said that the steps of black stone on which the monument is raised act as a barometer. If they bear signs of damp, as if they have recently been washed, then a change in the weather is on the way.

Withyham almost lost its church in 1663 when a fire partly destroyed the building. The parish register was blunt about the disaster, stating that on 'June ye 16, was Wytheham Church burnt down by a tempest of thunder and lightning.'

The Sackvilles, who were eventually driven away from Withyham because of the bad state of the roads, included two poets in the family. Thomas Sackville, born a second cousin to Queen Elizabeth I in 1536, is credited with reintroducing melody into English verse a century and a half after it had ceased with Chaucer. Charles Sackville, Sixth Earl of Dorset, was one of the more rakish pals of Charles II whose behaviour apparently scandalised Mr Pepys. But he was a great patron of men of letters and had the knack of writing graceful and lively verse himself. He went on to become Lord Chamberlain in the household of William of Orange.

It was the custom on the birthdays of the Earl and Countess De La Warr to fire a salute across the lake in Buckhurst Park from their private battery of 14 guns. Only seven of the guns were fired when any of their children had a birthday except in the case of the eldest son, Lord Buckhurst, who had the full battery blaze away in his honour. The de la Warr children used to delight in using the guns for target practice but their aim was sometimes wayward. After a shot had penetrated as far as Hartfield High Street the Earl intervened and the battery was silenced forever, the children presumably settling for the more mundane but safer candles on a birthday cake.

Wivelsfield 🦚

The Royal Oak was the scene of a celebrated murder on May 26th, 1734. Money was the motive behind the dark deed, because a Jewish pedlar called Jacob Harris overheard the landlord Richard Miles boasting that the inn had made a profit of £20 that week, a small fortune to a wanderer like Harris.

The pedlar murdered the landlord, his wife and a serving wench but the authorities soon caught up with him. He had hidden in a chimney at The Cat, West Hoathly, but tumbled out when someone lit the fire to dry their clothes. Harris was hanged on August 31st and his body left to hang on the gibbet near the pub as a practical warning to others. The area is still known as Jacobs Post.

A piece of the gibbet was held by country people for years afterwards to be a good luck charm and a defence against, amongst other things, an attack of toothache. The last remaining piece of this much picked-at gibbet still hangs in the bar at the Royal Oak.

From foul deeds to fair. Three brothers from Lincolnshire established Allwood's Carnation Nurseries at Wivelsfield Green in 1910 and achieved worldwide fame. A species of the Sweet William raised in the 1930s is named the Sweet Wivelsfield. The nurseries moved in 1960, the land was sold and is now a housing estate.

Great Ote Hall, a 15th century manor house acclaimed as one of the finest of that era in the county, was once the home of Selina Shirley, Countess of Huntingdon. This remarkable and determined woman was converted to the cause of evangelical Methodism by her sister-in-law and gave her chaplain the specific job of proclaiming her views to the world. When she came here in the middle of the 18th century one of the rooms was supplied with a pulpit from which her chaplain, the Rev W. Romaine, would preach. This was not enough for Selina and in 1778 she built Wivelsfield's Ote Hall Chapel, one of several churches in the county she used her wealth to build and known as the Countess of Huntingdon's Connection.

She seems to have run into a little religious rivalry in Wivelsfield. Two years after the construction of her chapel the Baptists built their own nearby. So together with the Norman church, what is essentially still a small farming community has three places of worship.

Another resident of Great Ote Hall was General Shirley, who became Commander-in-Chief of the forces in North America when it was still a British colony. He was either a proud man or a heavy one: It is said he never left home without six horses to his carriage.

Anglo Saxon Wifel's field had a grander title, though a sarcastic one, when the London to Brighton railway line was being built in the early years of Victoria's reign. It was boom time for the post office and shop, which used to be in a cottage next to the church, because the navvies would walk across the fields from the line to spend all their hard-earned cash. They called it 'going up to the city.'

Donkey derbies are now an established British tradition. The first one in the country was held here in 1951 and the story behind it is a fascinating one.

It was a wet day in the hay-making season and farmer Jim Dinnage was drowning his sorrows at The Royal Oak. Outside the window he saw a donkey, forlorn and bedraggled in the rain. Mr Dinnage felt so sorry for the beast that he bought it on the spot from the local rag and bone man which meant taking on the business 'lock, stock and barrel.' He arrived home with the donkey and a cartful of junk.

The donkey, a jack christened Billy, grew lonely for a mate in a way which upset the neighbours. He would bray at 3am and wander off into people's gardens. On one occasion he was brought back to Lone Barn Farm handcuffed to the irate local constable. So farmer Dinnage travelled to an abattoir in London where 13 donkeys were awaiting slaughter, part of a cruel trade in which the animals were exported from Ireland under terrible conditions and sold as veal during the post-war meat shortage. The farmer bought the lot and Billy got a new name – Lone Barn Farouk because of his harem of 13 wives.

He persuaded 12 of his friends at Wivelsfield to each take a moke, they jokingly called themselves The Donkey Club and hit on the bright idea of staging a donkey race meeting to help raise funds to pay for the purchase of the playing field. It was a great success, but it was felt more donkeys were needed. Soon afterwards Mr Dinnage saw a newspaper report which said 194 of the animals were running loose at Ashford after breaking out of a train bound for the slaughterhouse.

The International League for the Protection of Horses said it would buy the donkeys but desperately needed somewhere to keep them. They came to Lone Barn Farm amid a blaze of publicity and the offers to adopt a donkey and become members of The Donkey Club (at five shillings for life). It became a charity and at the second donkey derby a staggering 23,000 people poured into the village.

A host of celebrities started to give their support to the annual races, among them in the early years Laurel and Hardy, Gert and Daisy and Charlie Chaplin. A special coach used to take the distinguished visitors around the playing field to allow the crowd to get a good look and proceeds went to local charities.

Tragedy struck the Dinnage family in 1956 when their son Peter died of cancer at the age of 13. This prompted them to establish a holiday home by the sea at Lancing for the short-term care of the severely handicapped, and donkey derby profits were channelled into this. But when Jim Dinnage died in 1963 his widow Susan was forced to sell the holiday home. She put the proceeds into the building of a hospice at Lone Barn Farm, a caring place which can accommodate 25 residents and named St Peter's and St James's after her late son and husband. There are still donkeys there, a delight for residents and visitors alike.

The donkey derbies, too, are a well established part of village life every Spring Bank Holiday Monday. They are run now by Burgess Hill Round Table, the proceeds being shared equally by the hospice and the Table's charities.

Index